INTRODUCTION

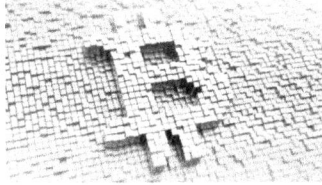

Bitcoin is without a doubt the most important invention since the Internet. In fact, it may even be bigger than the Internet. It is such a profound paradigm shift in the technology of money that even experts on the topic are still trying to wrap their heads around it.

In this book you will discover what Bitcoin is, how it works and why this technological breakthrough introduced in 2008 has the potential to radically transform humanity.

Bitcoin can be hard to grasp at first – and if someone has tried to explain it to you and you still feel like you just don't get it, don't worry. This book will take you by the hand and explain to you in the simplest terms, using analogies and metaphors what the essence of Bitcoin is and why you must pay attention to it.

You are about to embark on a fascinating journey that will open your eyes to the revolutionary technology that is Bitcoin.

INTRODUCTION

Bitcoin is without a doubt the most important invention since the Internet. In fact, it may even be bigger than the Internet. It is such a profound paradigm shift in the technology of money that even experts on the topic are still trying to wrap their heads around it.

In this book you will discover what Bitcoin is, how it works and why this technological breakthrough introduced in 2008 has the potential to radically transform humanity.

Bitcoin can be hard to grasp at first – and if someone has tried to explain it to you and you still feel like you just don't get it, don't worry. This book will take you by the hand and explain to you in the simplest terms, using analogies and metaphors what the essence of Bitcoin is and why you must pay attention to it.

You are about to embark on a fascinating journey that will open your eyes to the revolutionary technology that is Bitcoin.

A BRIEF HISTORY OF CRYPTOCURRENCY

Cryptocurrency began with the bitcoin as we all know. But did you know bitcoin was actually created in 2008 by Satoshi Nakamoto. And a side note is, Satoshi Nakamoto is actually not his real name. Smart guy! And there are some cryptocurrency circles who believe the name might actually stand for a small group of two or three people.

An interesting fact that doesn't have to stay a fact is that only

40% of bitcoin holders are over the age of 35! This was as of 2015. The rest were younger! Bitcoin is a finite resource as are all cryptocurrencies. And the mining of bitcoin will be done sometime in 2140.

While that is a 40 years into the future, this gives us a unique perspective as to the longevity that bitcoin is supposed to survive. For investors, that is a good point to notice. If bitcoin continues to be mined, then bitcoin most likely will continue to grow in some capacity of value. And as it becomes more scarce, will it too cause the value to rise?

"Bitcoin is following principles of economics and principles of market efficiency," says Hemang Subramanian, assistant professor in Florida International University's business information systems department. "It is an asset that is not controlled by a central entity, that is secure, international and fungible, liquid and is available in a limited supply for trade. This demand at near-constant supply has caused prices to go up disproportionately in a short period of time, attracting more investors."[1]

How many of you know why Mr. Nakamoto invented the bitcoin? What happened in 2008 in the financial world? This trickled down to all of us. People lost homes who had inflated mortgages. Banks received the biggest bailout in history. Did you? Or are you too young.

Bernard Maddoff pulled off the biggest Ponzi scheme ever in 2008. And the investment world reeled from this scheme. People lost everything How in the world could someone pull off that kind of investment scam? It could not be done with cryptocurrency. In 2008, millions were lost because they didn't actually exist. It was all a big lie.

We heard stories of young brokers who spent their first and last day on Wallstreet back in 2008. The biggest crash and global crisis since the Great Depression happened that year.

And one positive result of that terrible event was the creation of the bitcoin by Mr. Nakamoto. He was determined to create a method of exchange that did not depend on banks or the volatile Market. His goal was to create currency that people themselves controlled.

Go back just a little further to when bitcoin was created, it was not publicly available. However, when it was publicly available in 2009, if you were to buy $1000 dollars of bitcoin and weather the storms, you would now have over $36.7 million dollars.

Let's keep on the travel journey to when bitcoin was first traded. Did you know it was traded for pizza?! In 2010, someone actually traded in 10,000 of their bitcoin shares for 2 pizzas. Oh, to be that pizza owner! You would be so rich today! Just multiply 36.7 million, times ten. And the sap who thought pizza was more valuable than 10,000 bitcoin? It's called kicking yourself today and you know he is. YOU KNOW HE IS!

The Recorded Cryptocurrency History Timeline of Events:

1. The first Bitcoin was officially named by Nakamoto actually made a transaction in 2009. Bitcoin software then became available to the public and mining then became a "thing." New bitcoins were made and verified on this blockchain. By the way, Nakamoto is not his or "their" real name. No one knows who he/she or they are.

2. Next, the programmer Laszlo Hanyecz made the first recorded purchase for the two pizzas. And everyone knows his name! At the time, the purchase was worth about 40 bucks. It would now be about 90 million dollars. May 22, 2010 is known as the Bitcoin Pizza Day! This was the first event for bitcoin to have ever received a value.

3. During the year 2011, bitcoin gained popularity and the popularity of decentralization of funds began to catch on. Altcoins began to also come into the scene

and tried to attract people who would want to get in on another ground floor investment. They would try to improve the bitcoin basics with anonymity, speed, and other attractive features. Now we have over 5000 altcoins beside the original bitcoin!

4. In 2013, the bitcoin price collapsed. Not the price of 2 pizzas, but none the less, the price dove to $300 per coin. It would be over two years for bitcoin to rise again up over $1000.

5. The impossible feat happened. In Japan, the bitcoin was hacked in February of 2014. Hundreds of thousands of bitcoins worth millions were missing. Fortunes were lost. The Tokyo exchange filed for bankruptcy just after this event.

6. The Ethereum network was launched in July of 2015. This brought a smart contract to the digital currency world. A smart contract is a contract that is a code that controls digital assets.

7. In November of 2017, the value of the bitcoin reached $10,000. Then by the beginning of 2018, the bitcoin reached $19,000. In the meantime, for the past two years, bitcoin had been attracting investors from all over the world. The value had gradually increased over time and then of course, in December, the bitcoin made the front page of every newspaper.

8. Bitcoin spiked again in 2019 and cryptocurrencies multiplied exponentially. Facebook and other organizations hatched plans to launch digital exchanges which they did introduce in 2020, called Libra.

Now you have the brief history of cryptocurrency. An entire book could be written on just the history of cryptocurrency. But you didn't buy the history of cryptocurrency! You wanted to join the Crypto-Generation! This book is going to guide you and show you how right now!

UNDERSTANDING BITCOIN

What is Bitcoin

Bitcoin is a system of electronic peer-to-peer cash that is…

Open: Anyone can participate regardless of race, age, gender, political views…

Decentralized: No central party owns or controls it.

Censorship-resistant: Anyone can do whatever they want with their money and it is impossible to stop transactions on the network.

Permissionless: Anyone can innovate on top of Bitcoin without the need for anyone's permission.

Borderless: Bitcoin can be used anywhere in the universe as long as there is a connection to the network.

Bitcoin is a breakthrough in the field of computer science. In 2008, a person under the pseudo name Satoshi Nakamoto published a whitepaper stating that he had found a solution to the Byzantine General's problem, which is a problem in computer science for which there was no known solution. Satoshi's invention solved the problem of creating a decentral-ized network capable of achieving consensus without the inter-ference of any central authority. This technical exploit is what gave birth to Bitcoin. To this day, Satoshi's identity is unknown as he suddenly disappeared from the forums on which he was actively discussing Bitcoin with other early adopters. In 2011, he said that "he moved on other things" and has since then vanished from the Internet. Many people believe he may be dead but we will probably never be able to confirm this. Part of the magic surrounding Bitcoin is the fact that the inventor is a complete mystery.

At its core, Bitcoin is:

An invention just like the light bulb.

A technology just like the Internet.

A protocol just like TCP/IP.

Bitcoin isn't a company or an organization just like the Internet isn't a company. And no, Bitcoin.com doesn't own or control Bitcoin. It is merely the website of an early adopter that shares his own opinions about Bitcoin. Bitcoin is an open source protocol that is maintained by voluntary developers all over the world that freely contribute to the project. This is the same open source development methodology that was employed to build the Internet.

This can be hard to grasp at first. The idea of money not being owned and controlled by anyone is completely alien to our current society. Bitcoin operates through simple mathematical rules that participants agree upon. This allows it to emerge as the first decentralized network of computers that has the ability to reach consensus on what transactions have occurred on the network, therefore agreeing on who has how much money, and then recording this information on the blockchain, which we'll dive into later.

Make no mistake. Satoshi Nakamoto's invention is more important than just money. Money is merely first application. What Satoshi invented is a decentralized consensus system. He did this by solving the Byzantine General's problem we discussed earlier. This invention will allow us to build other applications that would have been unthinkable in the past.

With Bitcoin, for the first time in history, ownership of money isn't necessarily tied to a human being. Software can now own money. Just imagine a self-driving car that owns Bitcoins and that is programmed to give rides to people, earn money, pay its own fuel and taxes and then send back the profits to the owner. This is just one of the thousands of applications that will be possible with this new technology. Pandora's box has been opened and there is no going back.

Most people come across the idea of Bitcoin exclusively through the currency aspect of it. They hear about the price rising or falling down. Many people get into Bitcoin and other cryptocurrencies to get rich and then exit the markets. Don't get caught up in all this price action. It's mostly just noise. What's important is to deeply understand what Bitcoin is and why it's going to transform society. From such a place of understanding, it will be a lot easier to handle your investments in the long term.

Bitcoin Vs. Blockchain

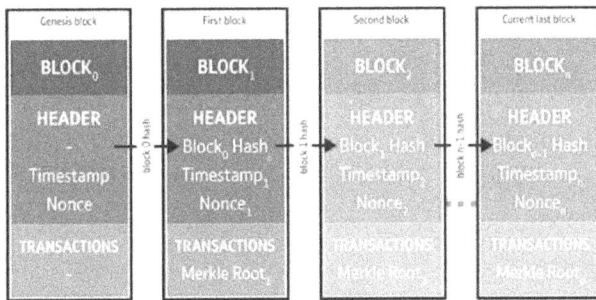

Representation of the Bitcoin Blockchain

If you've come across Bitcoin before, you may have heard the following phrases:

"The blockchain is the technology behind Bitcoin"

"The blockchain is more important than Bitcoin"

These ideas are completely incorrect. The Blockchain is one of the core technologies behind Bitcoin but it cannot in any way stand by itself.

A blockchain is simply a list of linked records or blocks that contain transaction data. The word blockchain could be used to describe a database that adds new blocks on top of previous ones. In Bitcoin, however, the blockchain that is utilized has specific characteristics that make it useful and unique. If you dissociate the blockchain from Bitcoin and its characteristics, you end up with a centralized database with signatures, which we had long before Bitcoin came along. There is no innovation there. Saying the blockchain is what really matters is like saying in 1992 that the Intranet (a private internet) is more important than the Internet.

The Bitcoin blockchain is public, open, decentralized, border-less, censorship-resistant and permission-less. The blockchain without Bitcoin doesn't work and Bitcoin without the blockchain also doesn't work.

The media loves to talk about blockchain technology because the powers at be don't want to deal with the disruptive nature of Bitcoin – they are starting to recognize it as serious threat to governments and banks and thus it is much easier for them to consider blockchain as a viable technology rather than Bitcoin.

Whenever you're presented with something that calls itself a blockchain, check to see if you can replace the word blockchain with database and see if the brochure reads the same. If it does, it's just business as usual. There is no disruption there.

How mining works

Bitcoin Mining Facility
In order to really understand Bitcoin, it is imperative to

grasp the concept of mining. Let's look at what happens when one makes a transaction on the Bitcoin network.

If Susan opens her Bitcoin wallet and sends money to Jeff, her transaction goes into what is called the mempool, which is essentially a repository of all the transactions waiting to be confirmed by the miners and subsequently added to the Bitcoin blockchain.

From there, the miners engage in a game-theoretical race where they assemble a block using the transactions in the mempool and format it according to the rules defined by the Bitcoin protocol.

In this process, they define how much Bitcoin they will be rewarded if they win the race. This is called the miner reward and it is explicitly defined in the protocol and designed to halve every four years. Satoshi chose to have this decreasing supply over time in Bitcoin to mimic the way gold is mined (as time passes, it becomes harder and harder to find gold and more energy is spent to find less and less gold.) The miner reward started at 50 Bitcoins in 2009 and will halve until the limit of 21 million Bitcoins is reached.

Once a miner assembles a block and formats it correctly, he now has to solve a mathematical problem using expensive hardware that consumes tremendous amounts of electricity. The first miner to find a solution wins the race and now has to attach that solution to his block and broadcast it to the entire network for confirmation. This solution itself can be used to mathematically prove that a certain amount of energy was spent to create it. This way, anyone can verify that a miner propagating a block has skin in the game.

Remember that miners everywhere in the world were also in the process of trying to find a solution to the problem. They suddenly receive a block that has been solved. They realize they have lost the race and immediately stop everything they are doing to verify the received block against the protocol rules and confirm its validity.

Is the block correctly formatted? Is the miner reward too high? Is the transaction valid? Is the miner trying to cheat the system?... Using cryptography, miners also check that the solution to the problem is valid and this way they prove that a certain amount of energy was spent to create this solution. This is called Proof of Work. It is a system that was invented by Adam Back in 1997 to fight email spam and it is at the heart of the Bitcoin technology.

The process of mining can be likened to a race to solve a Sudoku problem whereby just having a solved Sudoku is proof that someone must have spent time and energy to generate that solution, assuming the initial input of the Sudoku is random. This is what makes Bitcoin the most secure technology on the planet and this is what makes its blockchain the closest thing to immutability there is. It's basically backed by thermodynamics and the laws of the universe. In order to go back and change the last 100 blocks for instance, you would have to solve the problem mentioned earlier 100 times within a 10-minute period and present it to the network. This is simply unfeasible.

This results in a system where miners vote in a decentralized way and reach consensus on the validity of a block that is broadcasted to the network.

If a majority of miners vote the block to be valid, then it is confirmed and added to the blockchain. The transactions in that block are validated and in theory become immutable. If you received money from another person, you can rest assured that it won't just disappear.

If a majority of miners vote the block to be invalid for whatever reason (a miner trying to reward himself an incorrect amount or someone trying to spend their coins twice) the block is rejected and the miner that broadcasted it loses the time and energy he put into solving the mathematical problem.

From there, another race begins and the process repeats itself forever. This system of Proof Work is one of the core technologies of Bitcoin. Without it, there is no Bitcoin. Proof of Work ensures an unparalleled level of security to the system.

It is worth noting that the mining difficulty of Bitcoin is regularly adjusted at the protocol level so that it always takes on average 10 minutes to find a new block. As miner equipment becomes more and more efficient, difficulty is regulated to keep Bitcoin ticking about every 10 minutes.

If you've been exposed long enough to the subject of Bitcoin, you may have heard concerns about a 51% network attack on the Proof of Work system. This is the classic attack vector that is often presented as the Bitcoin killer. What if 51% or more of miners collude and overtake the voting system of Bitcoin? Even in such a scenario, it turns out such an attack may disrupt the network for a few blocks, but will eventually fail because it requires a ginormous amount of energy to sustain. Bitcoin has reached a level of computing that makes it impossible for even nation states to attack it successfully.

Proof of Work allows you to own your Bitcoin and be certain that nobody can take it away from you. This is unlike any other system in the world. Even with a bank account, the government can at any point seize your money and do whatever they like with it. Don't believe me? Look at what happened in the Cyprus crisis in 2013 when banks seized their customer's deposits to mitigate the crisis.

The concept of mining creates a scenario where it becomes dangerous to mess with the consensus rules of Bitcoin. Imagine you want to become a miner. You go out and invest tens of thousands of dollars in mining equipment and facilities. Then you hook that equipment to a megawatt incoming power source and you start mining. You make a profit from the mining rewards but you have to pay most of it to electricity bills. If you don't follow the rules of consensus, you don't get the miner reward but you still have to pay those electricity bills. Trying to game the system quickly leads to bankruptcy.

The incentive system in Bitcoin is setup so that it is more profitable to mine Bitcoin than to attack the network. The Bitcoin blockchain is constructed with this careful balance between risk and reward. Without it, Bitcoin is worth absolutely nothing. It would be vulnerable to attacks and would be taken over and controlled by a private entity. This is why talking about the blockchain without Bitcoin is like talking about the light bulb without electricity but with kerosene. Or the automobile without gasoline but with horses. We already have those. You can't do the light bulb without electricity. You can't do automobiles without gasoline and you can't do the blockchain without Bitcoin.

The Bitcoin blockchain has a set of rules engraved at the protocol level. One of those rules is that the issuance of Bitcoin cannot exceed 21 millions. This is a fixed cap that cannot be changed unless there is consensus in the network to do so. This is what makes Bitcoin valuable - supply is fixed, just like gold and unlike fiat currency that can be printed into oblivion by central banks.

Once all 21 million Bitcoins have been mined, mining will still continue to secure the network and validate transactions. However, miners will get rewarded solely on transaction fees (small fee users pay when sending a transaction), not on mining rewards, so the incentive will still be there for them to secure the network.

How the value of Bitcoin is determined

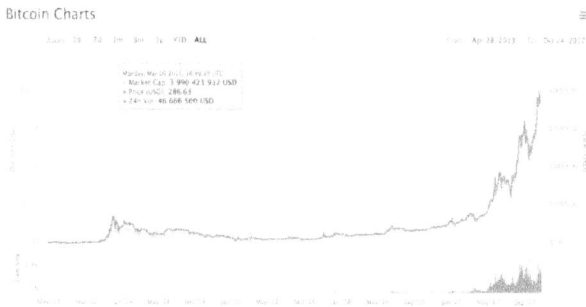

Bitcoin Price Evolution from April 2013 to October 2020

Many people new to Bitcoin wonder how its price is determined. It's actually very simple. Bitcoin price works exactly like a foreign currency.

Let's consider how the price of an apple determined. The price of an apple can be derived from two things: How much one is trying to sell it for, and how much one is trying to buy it for. As soon as there is a match between those two, price discovery occurs.

The value or price of Bitcoin is simply determined by demand and offer dynamics just like with any other currency. At any point in time there are millions of people buying and selling most currencies. While you might observe your local currency to be stable, its value is actually continually changing. One day you may have to pay 1.5 units of your local currency to buy 1 Euro for instance, but the next day you may have to pay 2 units. Bitcoin works precisely the same way. The market determines the price through supply and demand dynamics. As Bitcoin adoption grows and more people use Bitcoin, the price will continue to go up in the long-term.

Why Bitcoin will change the world

Bitcoin allows us to do things we could have never dreamed of in the past:

1. For the first time in history, populations under the oppres-

sion of corrupt legal systems and irresponsible monetary poli-
cies have a way to exit the system and protect their assets from
theft and hyperinflation. This is already happening in countries
like Venezuela and Argentina.

2. For the first time in history, people can safely store their
money without it being subject to risky speculation by the
banking system. Bitcoin offers the possibility for anyone in the
world to have the equivalent of a Swiss bank inside his pocket.

3. For the first time in history, anyone in the world can pay
any other person almost instantly no matter where they are on
the planet without a middleman, paying only a few cents in
transaction fees.

4. For the first time in history, merchants can accept electronic payments without a third party middleman that takes a
percentage of every transaction.

5. Other important applications are yet to be seen on the
Bitcoin network. Bitcoin is at a similar stage as the Internet was
in the early 90's. Mind blowing applications will be built on top
of the base protocol just like social media was built on top of the
Internet. The future is bright and nearly impossible to predict.

Top Bitcoin Myths

Although Bitcoin has been around since 2009, there still exist
widespread misconceptions that prevent people from getting
started with it. The fact that Bitcoin is a complex subject that
requires a basic understanding of several different areas also
helps to perpetuate these myths. Here are 7 common myths
about Bitcoin dismantled:

Myth #1: Bitcoin is Dead

This is perhaps the most common myth about Bitcoin. That it
is dead for good and no longer used by anybody in the world.
There is a website called 99Bitcoins which has a page called
Bitcoin Obituaries that keeps track of the declarations of
Bitcoin's death dating back to 2010. As of the time of writing this
book, Bitcoin has "died" 179 times. Yet Bitcoin is at its most

successful point in history with more transactions happening on the network than ever and with scaling solutions being successfully deployed.

Myth #2: Bitcoin is only used by terrorists and criminals

The media likes to paint the picture that Bitcoin is exclusively used by criminals. This idea echoes Jamie Dimon's (CEO of JPMorgan) recent statements about Bitcoin where he insisted that it is a fraud worse than tulip bulbs and that it is only useful if you are a criminal. Meanwhile, there is no evidence of Bitcoin being used by terrorists on a meaningful scale. The reality is that Bitcoin is still more traceable than cash since the public blockchain records all the transactions. For terrorists looking to make untraceable payments, cash is still king.

Myth #3: Bitcoin's volatility makes it useless

While it is true that Bitcoin has a history of volatility with some impressive price swings, this trend has been declining since 2009. Bitcoin is used at the moment as a store of value more than anything else. As time goes on, this volatility will inevitably become more and more insignificant and it will become almost impossible for any entity to significantly affect the price of Bitcoin.

Myth #4: Bitcoin is a ponzi scheme

A ponzi scheme requires an initial founder to convince investors to get in by promising some sort of return. In Bitcoin, no one makes such a promise. A ponzi requires a constant stream of new investors to pay earlier investors. Bitcoin can continue working without more users. If one reaches the conclusion that Bitcoin is a ponzi scheme, then there is no choice but to also recognize that all currencies in the world and even gold are merely ponzi schemes.

Myth #5: The CEO of Bitcoin was arrested

In 2013, the anonymous online black market Silk Road was shut down by the FBI and in 2014, the exchange Mt Gox went bankrupt due to insolvency. Many people new to Bitcoin have interpreted these events to mean that Bitcoin was shut down in 2013 or that it collapsed in 2014. This is due to an inability to distinguish between the companies and services built on top of Bitcoin and the Bitcoin protocol itself. Of course, Silk Road and Mt Gox had their CEOs both arrested but Bitcoin has no CEO.

Myth#6: Bitcoin isn't backed by anything so it can't have real value

This comes from a fundamental misunderstanding of what money really is. Throughout history, we have used feathers, stones and now paper as money because money is simply an abstraction that allows us to communicate value more easily. Since 1971, paper money is no longer backed by gold. Moreover, it can be inflated into oblivion by governments. Thus, fiat currencies we have today technically don't have much value. Bitcoin has value because it is a scarce asset that is extremely difficult to obtain.

Myth #7: Bitcoin is anonymous

Bitcoin is often thought of the anonymous currency of the dark web criminals. The reality is that Bitcoin is pseudonymous. There is a public address for each wallet in the network but no one can know who is really behind this address. With Bitcoin, every transaction that is made is available on the public blockchain and anyone can inspect it using an online block explorer. This will change in the future as more innovations are built on top of Bitcoin to allow for completely anonymous transactions.

The evolution of money

This chapter is meant to give you a bit of perspective on how money has evolved over the years and how Bitcoin is merely a natural step forward in the evolution of money.

At the most basic level, a way to communicate value is to exchange things that are considered to be of equal value. Exchanging a chicken for 20 bananas may have been one of the first transactions in history, even though it's a barter transaction that isn't using money.

We then moved from barter to the first abstract forms of money where people started exchanging something you can't consume (a feather, a bead, some metal) for something of value.

One of the most popular forms of this abstraction was precious metals because they have some of the most important characteristics of money: scarce, easy to transport and easy to divide. This transition to precious metals took hundreds of thousands of years.

A few thousand years later, someone came up with the idea of paper money. If one deposits gold with a trusted third party and receives a piece of paper that proves the existence of the gold, then the paper can be traded instead of the gold. This idea was met with a tremendous amount of skepticism and resistance at the time. If you think Bitcoin is weird, imagine how people felt when they suddenly had to trust a piece of paper instead of gold. It took approximately 400 years for paper to be accepted as money.

About 60 years ago, a new form of money emerged in the form of plastic cards. The first credit card was actually a traveler's cheque. People were again skeptical and preferred to receive paper money instead!

Today, we have Bitcoin. A technical breakthrough in the technology of money. Perhaps more radical than the shift from precious metals to paper money. Bitcoin is an invention that transforms the oldest technology in civilization. It disrupts the very architecture of money where each participant is now equal. In Bitcoin, you can be your own bank and no one can censor you. This innovation is scary to a lot of people because it renders banks obsolete and causes governments to lose the power they have amassed through their ability to control the money supply.

Influencers to follow

To deepen your knowledge of Bitcoin, there are some key

influencers that you may want to follow to stay up to date with the latest information around Bitcoin:

Andreas Antonopoulos

Technologist and serial entrepreneur who has become one of the most well known and respected figures in Bitcoin. Author of 'Mastering Bitcoin', which goes into the technical aspects of Bitcoin. One of the most engaging speakers in Bitcoin. Can be found on Twitter.

Simon Dixon

CEO and cofounder of online investment platform BnkTo-TheFuture.com

An ex-investment banker turned Bitcoiner and author of 'Bank to the Future'.

Simon is an active Bitcoin angel investor who appears in much of the major media including BBC, FT, CNBC, Bloomberg and Wall Street Journal. Can be found on Twitter.

World Crypto Network

Number one Bitcoin show on YouTube specialized in covering all things related to Bitcoin and cryptocurrencies. Regular updates every week on the current state of Bitcoin.

Tone Vays

Derivatives Trader & Consultant in the realm of Economics, Finance, Blockchain and Bitcoin. Can be found on YouTube under Tone Vays and also on Twitter.

Max Keiser

American broadcaster and filmmaker. Hosts the Keiser Report, a financial program broadcast on the Russian state media channel RT that features unorthodox economics theories. Can be found on Twitter.

CrushTheStreet

YouTube show specialized in unconventional financial news and trends. Covers Bitcoin regularly.

◆◆◆

Bitcoin is a new type of currency, of the like the world has never experienced. It is completely new, revolutionary, and is becoming a household name. Though it has greatly increased in value since its birth in 2009, it's still in its infancy. This is because, as I'll be discussing in this book, there is still much growth to be had in Bitcoin. If you didn't become a millionaire by buying $10 worth of Bitcoin in 2009 and keeping it until today, it's okay! It's not too late. While I can't promise that you'll be a millionaire, I will say that there is a potential profit windfall to be made if you get into Bitcoin in the near future. So without further ado, let's go over why Bitcoin is the future, why it's here to stay, and why its price will skyrocket in the near future!

WHAT IS BITCOIN

While there is a lot of background to Bitcoin which includes blockchain, the ledger, mining, etc., the main point to understand is Bitcoin is a digital currency that can be used as a form of payment and a store of value. A Bitcoin itself is not a physical item, but a number on a screen, that was essentially created out of thin air. Knowing this, you may think to yourself "well why the heck would I invest in that?" But hold on young grasshopper! The value of many things are created out of thin air. It's what the public preserves as the worth of something that gives it its value. Let's take for example diamonds. Diamonds are useless rocks made of carbon that happened to be smooshed in the ground the right way over many millions of years, and are thus arranged in a special formation. Aside from very limited tasks, diamond is essentially useless, and its value has been arrived upon by humans stating it should be worth something. You can thank the De Beers company for this, as they essentially started the diamond trend in the early 1900's with a magnificent amount of marketing, and now hold a monopoly on the industry.

A US dollar is also completely useless. It's a piece of paper that has no physical use, yet a US bill that says $100 on it is worth 100x more than one that says $1 on it. Why is this? It's because the citizens of the United States, as well as much of the world, have accepted it as a form of currency, and thus use it as such.

Everything in this world that has value gets that value from the congregation of the masses giving it said value. It's what people have agreed upon and the way the world operates. As such, just because Bitcoin was "created out of thin air" doesn't mean it isn't worth something. The world is starting to see the value in Bitcoin, which will soon allow it to become worth more and more as time goes on.

You see, money is a network. The more people that have said money and use it, the more valuable it is. Think of the first telephone that was ever created... pretty useless huh? You couldn't even call yourself. However, once a second telephone was created, it then became much more useful. And as more telephones were made and distributed, the telephone network became something others wanted to be a part of.

There is a concept known as Metcalfe's Law which states a network is as effective as the number of users it has in it squared (n^2). As such, the more people that acquire and start using Bitcoin, whether it be as a currency, store of value, or both, the more valuable the Bitcoin network will be. And as the media keep talking about Bitcoin, and the price of it keeps rising, the network will continue to grow, thus expanding itself more and more with time.

IMPORTANT TERMS FOR INVESTING

Primary Terms

There are several words or terms you should be familiar with if you are to understand cryptocurrency. Whether you plan to invest or just want to be educated in this wave of finance, these terms are essential for you to know. These are the main terms you will hear over and over again. While we define these terms in this chapter, you will have a much better under-standing of these terms as you read more about how they are used in a practical way in other chapters.

The more you know, the more you will be better prepared to invest.

These words are listed in alphabetical order and will be explained in depth both in this chapter and throughout the rest of this book as the need for their use entails.

1. Altcoin
2. Bitcoin
3. Blockchain
4. Flat
5. Mining
6. Private Key
7. Public Key or Address

Altcoin

The altcoin is sometimes described as an alternative to the bitcoin. This coin was designed to make up for flaws that showed up during the use of the bitcoin. Some users were unhappy with the bitcoin's speed, the shortcoming on the bitcoin's framework, whether it was actually a perception or not, and mining cost.

The altcoin also provided competition for the bitcoin and gave investors another place to get into the cryptocurrency system. A bonus to the altcoin is that it has a lower transaction fee. There are over 5000 altcoins in circulation and some of them are pure junk. In contrast, some altcoins do very well, such as Chainlink and Ethereum.

Some other examples of the altcoin are Litecoin, Dash, Ripple, NEM, and Monero. There are also altcoins designed to protect the stability of cryptocurrency. They are called stable coins. Some examples of those are tether and libra. Libra is on Facebook. To briefly sum up the altcoins; many are very new and the investment as such is risky.

Bitcoin

As stated in the introduction, "oh to have invested in the bitcoin in the beginning!" This author just talked to an investor who just bought a fraction of a bitcoin on December 31, 2020 for $700. A purchase made believing the bit coin value is going to continue to rise again.

Had the investor purchased the bitcoin with $700 even 2 years ago, he would have a tidy nest egg today. But what exactly is this bitcoin and what makes it the most attractive cryptocurrency even now? Even still, his investment is growing much faster than any stock or savings account right now.

The bitcoin for beginners is a bit hard to picture. It is not actually a coin. It is a more like a file you keep in a wallet, but not an actual wallet. This is a wallet you have on your computer or your phone.

This bitcoin file will register once you make a transaction. The transaction may be an input or an output but you will see the file on your computer or phone in your account. The bitcoin address from where the transaction was made will be included. Then the bitcoin should show up in your wallet in a key. A record of where money was sent and received is also included.

Free Bitcoin

If you want to get in the game of investing in bitcoin an easy way to start is to go onto Coinbase, which is rated the "Best Overall" and just register to invest. Once you are registered, they ask you upload a copy of your legal ID, and the website will actually give you $5 of bitcoin. That is a very small fraction down to 8 decimal points, but it's something!

After you have gone through those simple steps you are free to invest. On Coinbase as well as other investment sites, they

have multiple articles guiding and advising as to what investments may be the most lucrative. Bitcoin is the most heard of
cryptocurrency and most lucrative one to date as well.

Blockchain

When describing blockchain as a database, this is quite
frankly where we lose people. But stay with us. A blockchain is
very simply a database of how the cryptocurrency is formed and
a record of all the transactions of that currency. It's a history of
that currency.

A blockchain is what it says it is: a block of data formed to a
make a chain. Or formed on a chain. Every transaction that is
made is stored on the blockchain, which in theory should make
cryptocurrency less vulnerable for fraud or not easy to hack. The
blockchain should be very secure. (More will be written on the
blockchain in chapter 4)

Fiat

Fiat money is money that has been sanctioned by a government, meaning the value is guaranteed by a government in that
the government vouches for its worth. The seller and buyer
using fiat for a transaction using this in good faith understand
that when the exchange is made the currency will hold it's value
after the transaction is complete. The Euro is fiat money. The US
dollar is fiat money.

Mining

For this type of mining, you do not need a pan and a stream,
but we are still mining for gold so to speak! Mining for gold
might actually have been easier back in the day than mining for
cryptocurrency, but there are some people who are very good at
this skill and have earned bitcoins by mining. Usually, they are
either working for someone else or members of a pool.

To mine for cryptocurrency, it requires a tremendous amount
of electricity. The largest mining places are located in China and
in the Arctic Circle. Of course ,mining can be done elsewhere! It
involves solving a complex series of math problems and literally

mining the bitcoin out of those problems. People work together to solve those problems. In chapter VII, we discuss mining in depth. If mining is something you are interested in, you have come to the right place!

Private Key

The private key is your private key. If we are talking about bitcoin, your private key is the key to your bitcoin. It's your secured ownership. For example, you do not turn over the keys to your car and say, "Here you go!" That is the equivalent of saying, "Take my car."

By the same token, you do not give the numbers to your private access of your bitcoin key. It is a number used to represent your bitcoin or cryptocurrency when you make a transaction and open your wallet. Your private key is your key to your cryptocurrency.

Public Key

The public key sends an encryption to the person (the recipient) and then the person on the receiving end will use the private key to decrypt the message.

Secondary Terms Throughout This Book

The above vocabulary terms are the main ones you should know moving forward. There are more terms we will run across as we get further into our study of cryptocurrency. We will tackle those secondary terms as they arise.

Some people find definitions and vocabulary boring but you already know more than the average Joe about cryptocurrency by knowing these terms! And you've only a few pages into the new world of investing! You are more knowledgeable than most of the world right now about Cryptocurrency!

Our second chapter is going to take us through a quick history lesson of how we got where we are and why you can stop kicking yourself for not investing in bitcoin 2 years ago or worse, 3 years ago! For pennies! Yikes!

Ok, you can kick yourself once, but no more! This investment game is still very, very young and we can still make a lot of money! All the information is right here if cryptocurrency is your path of choice.

Bitcoin continues to gain in value. After a crash or two, bitcoin now has hit the highest value of all time. Today as these words are being typed, bitcoin is worth $35,983.60 USD. There are those who study the crypto who believe bitcoin may reach $60,000 by sometime in 2021. Still there are others who believe much higher.

What does this mean for you? As we have noted, you can buy portions of bitcoin if you have money to invest. The trust in bitcoin is coming from the investors in the community of bitcoin.

Cryptography

One more term to discuss separately is Cryptography. What is cryptography? This is the language of data. A cryptographer is someone who can convert ordinary plain text into text that is unable to be read or vice-versa. Cryptography protects against theft and against alteration.

The sender and the receiver have the same keys during a transaction and the receiver is able to unlock the code with the key and the message is decoded on the receiver's end. This is the way cryptography works.

To become a cryptographer, it usually takes 5 years for the degree in computer and information technology security. In the past, most of the jobs were found in the military, military organizations and government agencies. However, now cryptologists are needed in cyber security and various firms that deal in cryptocurrency. The pay in the private sector is considerably more than in the military.

The most famous cryptographer in the US Navy was also called The First Lady of Cryptology. He name was Agnes Meyer Driscoll. She served in both WWI and WWII as a Navy Cryptographer breaking codes in both wars for the United States. She was responsible for breaking Japan's codes, not once, but twice. The second time they started using machines for their next series of codes she was able to manually break the second series. When Driscoll died in 1971, she was buried in Arlington National Cemetery.

GETTING STARTED WITH BITCOIN

H ow to Buy and Secure Bitcoins

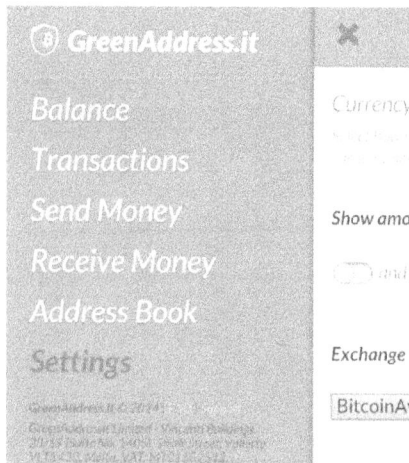

Green Address Wallet Interface on Android

Now that you have a basic understanding of what Bitcoin is, you may be tempted to go out and get yourself some

Bitcoin so you can start playing with this revolutionary technology.

The first step is choosing a wallet that will hold your Bitcoin. A Bitcoin wallet is essentially the equivalent of your "bank account". It allows you to receive Bitcoins using a Bitcoin address, store them and send them to other people. The big difference is that you hold your own private keys so no one on controls the contents of your wallet.

Here are some of the best wallets for beginners:

GreenAdress

Electrum

Samourai Wallet

Airbitz

These wallets all provide a high degree of security and allow you to own your private keys.

For further security, it is highly advised to upgrade to a hard-ware wallet, especially if you are holding a significant amount of value. A hardware wallet is basically a physical offline wallet that is much more difficult to hack. The two best hardware wallets are Nano ledger S and Trezor.

Keep in mind that exchanges like Coinbase or Bitfinex are not wallets. They allow you to store Bitcoins on their platforms but you are not in control of your private keys so you have to trust them with your value.

The next step is to actually go out and buy Bitcoins. There are two main ways to do this:

Use a Bitcoin exchange

A Bitcoin exchange is a company specialized in allowing its users to buy and sell Bitcoins. They offer liquidity to the market by making a large amount of Bitcoins available.

Here are some of the best exchanges out there:

Coinbase (US customers only)

Kraken

Bitstamp

Bitfinex
Poloniex

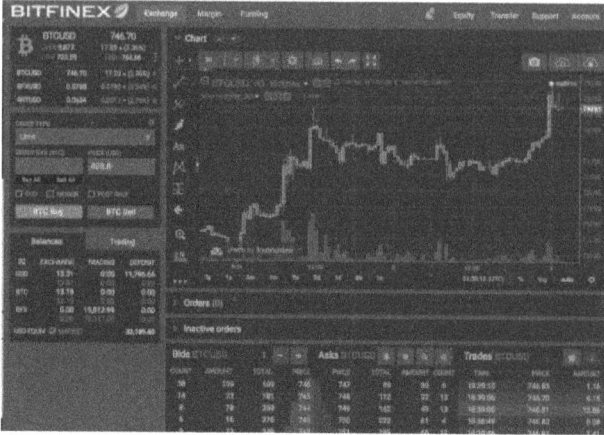

BITFINEX EXCHANGE INTERFACE: PEER TO PEER TRANSACTIONS

Another way to buy Bitcoin is to find someone that wants to sell
Bitcoins and offer to buy them. This isn't easy to do and it's the
reason why there are websites like localBitcoins.com that will
match you to an individual just like you that wants to sell or buy
Bitcoins. The website will handle the transaction using an
escrow service and thus make sure nobody cheats.

How to make money with Bitcoin

It's best not to treat Bitcoin as a get-rich-quick scheme. Only put money you are willing to lose into Bitcoin. It has a very high chance of success but that doesn't mean its risk free.

If you treat it exclusively as an investment, you will be more likely to panic sell when the price goes down and then buy out of fear of missing out when the price goes up. Moreover, unless you know exactly what you are doing, I would advise you to not trade Bitcoin. It's almost impossible to call a top or a bottom in Bitcoin and most traders end up losing money in this game.

View Bitcoin as a store of value instead of an investment where you are expecting a return and you will find it easy and stress free to be involved in it.

It has been shown time and time again that you do much better holding Bitcoin than trying to trade it or even trying to mine it. So buy and hold your Bitcoins unless you know exactly what you are doing.

Understanding Forks

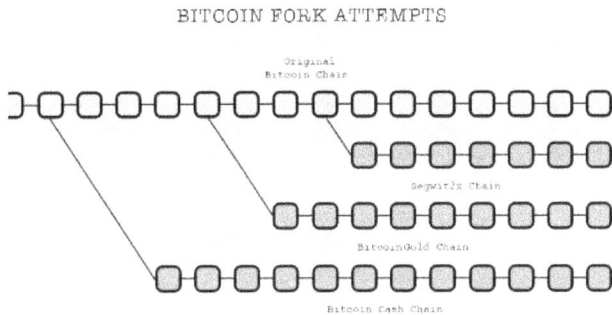

BITCOIN FORK ATTEMPTS

If you follow the news around Bitcoin, you may have heard of the concept of forks. In Bitcoin, a fork is a technical event that occurs whereby the state of the blockchain diverges into two distinct states. In such a scenario, part of the network has a different perspective on what a valid block is than the rest of the network.

Keep in mind that forks occur naturally in Bitcoin about

twice a week without anyone even noticing it. Remember the race in mining we talked about earlier? Imagine that two miners, miner A and miner B find a block at the same time and propagate it to the network at the same time.

One part of the network (closer to miner A) receives miner A's block and another part of the network receives miner's B block. Both blocks are valid, and this results in a temporary fork where two versions of the blockchain co-exist. This is because a portion of the miners has added the first block to the blockchain and the other has added the second block.

Both are valid and anyone that started mining on top of either block is not doing anything wrong. So the question remains, which block is going to extend the blockchain? We can't ask a central authority because we've taken that part out with Bitcoin.

As stated earlier, a new race now begins and miners start mining for the next block according to their individual perspective of the blockchain that is valid. After a few minutes, let's say that miner C finds a block before everyone else. It so happens that miner C had previously added the block from miner A to the blockchain. (when miner A and miner B found a block at the same time)

Miner C puts a link to the previous block he mined on top of (block from miner A) and propagates it to the network. Other miners in the network now have to build on top of the block from miner A and discard block from miner B because the chain with the block from miner A has become the longest chain. The fork is resolved and the blockchain goes back to a normal state where everyone agrees on the history of transactions.

What I just described is a fork that occurs without deliberate planning because of the very real probability of two miners finding a block around the same time. However there are other types of fork that are more deliberate where part of the network decides to change the rules in a way that may not be compatible with the rest of the network.

There are two types of deliberate forks:

Soft forks: With soft forks, rules become tighter. For example: Changing the block size limit from 1MB to 0.5 MB. In this scenario, a block that was previously valid can become invalid. A soft fork is backwards compatible so that new blocks that appear on the network are still valid by the old rules. Everyone can keep following the rules because the new blocks are still valid since they only have tighter specifications. This allows the introduction of new features without loosening the rules.

Hard forks: With hard forks, rules become looser. For example: Changing the block size limit from 1MB to 2 MB. In this scenario, a block that was previously invalid can become valid. A hard fork implies that certain blocks on the network will now be considered invalid by part of the network and they won't be able to participate with the new consensus rules unless they upgrade to the new rules. A hard fork forces participants to upgrade or be left behind.

To understand more deeply the concept of forks, let's consider the fictitious example of a free, decentralized public food stand. Let's say the stand starts out giving vegetarian meals only. Adding meat to the menu would be a hard fork because all of a sudden some people will consider the rules of the food stand no longer valid and they will have to find a different place to eat. Expanding the menu therefore requires consumers to upgrade their diet or go somewhere else. However, if cooks decided to turn the vegetarian recipe into a vegan recipe by taking out dairy for instance, then this is a soft fork. Everyone that is vegetarian can still eat vegan. The rules have been tightened.

The beautiful thing about Bitcoin is that for a fork to happen successfully, it requires the consensus of the developers, the miners, the merchants and the users. These parties must find overwhelming of consensus in order to change Bitcoin. This is the reason why Bitcoin is difficult to change. Segregated Witness, which is a soft fork upgrade and a scaling solution, took two years to be activated on the network because the miners didn't agree to the upgrade. This tension is a design principle of open blockchains, and it ensures that no entity no matter how well funded can hijack the system.

As a user, if a hard fork happens, you will automatically have funds on both sides of the fork assuming you are holding your own private keys.

HOW BITCOIN WILL TAKE OVER THE WORLD

C urrency wars
There is a fully-fledged, global currency war that is happening right now and it will be a source of tremendous growth for Bitcoin as billions of people fall victim to it and find a safe haven in Bitcoin.

This is happening already in counties like Greece, Cyprus, Spain, Venezuela, Brazil, Argentina, Turkey, India, Pakistan, Ukraine... which are currently, involved in domestic or international currency wars, where the citizens of these countries are held hostage to the reckless practices of their governments.

In India, towards the end of 2016, Prime Minister Modi announced with 4 hours notice that the two largest denominations of bills would no longer be valid. He instantly removed over 80% of the cash in circulation in a country where over 95% of the transactions happen in cash and where over 60% of people have no bank account. This demonetization created a disaster in India where many people of modest means became unable to buy food or pay for medical care.

This is an experiment that will repeat itself in other countries in the next few years. Governments all over the world aim to completely eradicate cash because it is the ultimate peer-to-peer form of money where transactions cannot be easily monitored and censored. Their dream is a future where only digital transactions can happen on platforms that allow for surveillance, control, confiscation and censorship. This can only be achieved once cash is completely eradicated.

Another form of currency wars is also already taking place. Governments desperate to pay back their international debt are using their own currency to erode this debt by inflating it into oblivion; essentially making their population indirectly pay for this debt. They print money, pay their debt and leave their population to deal with the consequences of the resulting inflation.

In the midst of all this chaos, there is for the first time in history an option that is completely neutral, an exit strategy for people all around the world to reclaim their freedom. That is Bitcoin, and it will be standing as a safe haven asset for billions of people around the world who are under the financial oppression of their own government.

Bitcoin is going to become a direct insult to sovereignty in many countries. This is happening already in countries like Venezuela where Bitcoin is illegal. The hyperinflation in Venezuela is causing citizens to mass exit their currency by exchanging it for Bitcoin. Many Venezuelans go on Amazon Pantry to buy groceries using Bitcoins, get them delivered at adjacent countries and illegally smuggle them into their country to feed their families.

Bitcoin is a blessing from the sky for those people. It is designed as money for the people and this is why it will completely transform society.

Unfortunately for them, all fiat currencies in the world are competing against Bitcoin. Thus, it's not merely about Bitcoin succeeding. It's about Bitcoin surviving while the entire financial system collapses.

Hyperbitcoinization

The term hyperbitcoinization refers to the possibility of Bitcoin induced currency demonetization, which is what can happen to any currency in the world as it forced to compete with Bitcoin and rapidly lose its value in the process.

Let's dive into the relationship between demonetization, hyperinflation and hyperbitcoinization.

Demonetization is a process by which people cease to use a currency unit as it is no longer legal tender. Hyperinflation, on the other hand can be seen as a type of demonetization where the government inflates the currency at an accelerating pace. This results in the currency having less and less value.

HyperBitcoinization is another kind of demonetization that looks similar. In both scenarios, prices in the original currency are inflated until the currency loses its utility.

HyperBitcoinization differs from hyperinflation in the following ways:

- A currency goes into hyperinflation without much competition with other currencies.
  HyperBitcoinization happens because of direct competition with Bitcoin. This is because Bitcoin is a borderless system whereas fiat currency is easily be subject to capital controls.
- In a hyperinflation event, the government has to increase the money supply in such a way to surpass people's expectations of future inflation in order to gain from the inflation. HyperBitcoinization, on the other hand does not need any change in supply.

HyperBitcoinization is essentially as process by which there is a deliberate transition from an inferior currency to a superior one, through a cascade of individual acts by people who look to exit their fiat currency and go with a superior, more stable form of money.

Alternative cryptocurrencies

If you have been in the Bitcoin space for more than a day, you probably have heard about alternative cryptocurrencies or "alt coins. " These are basically cryptocurrencies that have been developed by other people. There has been a tremendous boom in alt coins as the frenzy of the blockchain has intensified in the past few months.

Many Bitcoin experts and myself believe that we are in an altcoin bubble right now. The altcoin space is similar to the dotcom bubble back in 1998. There are many projects that promise you the moon, raise a ton of money and then proceed to accomplish exactly nothing with this money. Don't get me wrong, there are a few altcoins that may be useful in the future. Some are addressing completely different use cases from Bitcoin. However, if you're going to get into altcoins, thorough research is required to not get scammed in this space. There is still very little regulation for ICOs (Initial Coin Offerings) so scammers all over he world have flocked to this opportunity to make a quick buck.

Thank you for downloading this book! I hope it was able to help you understand the technology of Bitcoin in much greater depth.

Bitcoin is here to stay and hopefully by now I have convinced you of that. It will be as big as, and perhaps bigger than the Internet.

It will radically transform how we relate society and will yield many more innovations that will be built on top of the base protocol.

WHY BITCOIN WILL RULE ALL CRYPTOCURRENCIES

◆ ◆ ◆

There are many digital currencies springing up, or initial coin offerings (ICOs) as they are being called. The reason for this is, with the right technology, anyone can make a "digital coin." However just because a coin is made doesn't mean it's valuable or will be worth anything. I could also create my own paper currency, but I don't think anyone will trade "Morris" dollars. The reason why Bitcoin will remain king in the cryptocurrency world is because it was the first mover and has the most adoption behind it.

Remember, any cryptocurrency is valued based on what the public thinks it's worth. Considering Bitcoin was the first cryptocurrency to be made, and as such has the largest user base, it will ultimately have a strong hold on the industry. I don't truly think there will be 30 different crypto coins in the future people will be buying things with; that would get too confusing. As such, it is the only cryptocurrency I will be referencing in this book and the only one I would suggest going into.

WHY BITCOIN WILL SKYROCKET

◆ ◆ ◆

Inflation
In primitive times, humans used to use gold and silver as a means of currency. Everyone understood gold and silver had value, and as such, would accept it for items being sold. As governments became bigger, they began making their own currency, which was originally backed by some form of

commodity, as in gold or silver. As in they could only make as much currency as they had commodity in reserve, which meant it was backed by something, making it stable. Soon, governments began getting away from this premise, and instead of a commodity back currency, they just backed currency by the "word" of the government. In the United States for example, the Nixon administration removed the US from the gold standard in 1971.

Considering currencies were no longer backed by a commodity, as well as the rise of central banks like "The Fed" in the USA, governmental currencies could now go through what is known as inflation. This is where a $1 is worth less in a year than it is today. It's why a pack of gum would have cost you 10 cents fifty years ago, but costs $1.50 today. Unless you have your money invested in something that rises in value over time like stocks or gold, inflation is the reason why your money will slowly lose it's worth. While inflation hasn't impacted the United States as much as some other countries, it still has an effect on us. The average rate of inflation in the US each year is 3.22%. This means something that costs you $1 today will cost you $1.03 in one year. The primary reason behind inflation is because, since there is no commodity backing a currency, governments are able to print as much currency as they want. The issue then becomes that each additional dollar that goes into circulation devalues the overall worth of the currency. Before you know it, spending gets out of hand and currencies aren't worth the paper they are printed on.

Let's take a look at Venezuela, which is projected to have an inflation rate of 10,000,000% in 2019. As in something that costs one dollar today will cost $10,000,000 next year! Think this is bad, then why not look at Zimbabwe which experienced inflation of 89.7 sextillion percent (that's 21 zeros) in 2008. While this hasn't happened in the US, the potential is there, especially if other countries start asking to collect on the money they've loaned us. As the time of writing this book, the US government is 22.4 trillion dollars in debt, and I haven't heard one politician bring up paying our debt down in the latest presidential rallies. All they keep bringing up is spending more! There is an excellent documentary I highly suggest watching which is free on Amazon. That documentary is called *End of The Road* (fastlink.xyz/road). It has some very high level economists who go over this scenario in more detail, and what would happen if this countries did start collecting their debts from the United States.

What many people fail to realize is countries rise and fall, and their currency goes with them. The British pound is the oldest currency in existence, having an age of 317 years. However, this is an exception to the rule. The average lifespan of a fiat currency is just 27 years. As in most currencies fail and don't come back! Do you want your money in something with an average lifespan of 27 years? This statistic further proves that a currency backed by a country is in no way "safe," as many would like to believe.

I want to focus on Venezuela for a second though, as it shows us a very good example of why Bitcoin is so important. What was the first thing residents of Venezuela started using as currency once the Venezuelan Bolívar (the currency in Venezuela) started to hyperinflate? Did they start trading in gold and silver and copper coins? NO! They immediately started buying and selling in Bitcoin!

What this shows is Bitcoin is the new gold! It is the digital gold of the future. While gold made sense hundreds of years ago, Bitcoin makes sense now. You can store it on an app on your phone, and conveniently use it to pay for items at a variety of locations, of which more and more are accepting Bitcoin. Instead of having to make sure to have enough gold coins on you when you go places, you just need your phone. And when you pay, it automatically calculates the exact fraction of Bitcoin to take out of your Bitcoin wallet.

Lightning Network

Throughout much of Bitcoin's history, scalability has been a problem. As in, the number of users who could successfully use the network quickly, and in a timely manner. For many years, the Bitcoin network could process a max of 7 transactions per second. Compare this to Visa's average of 24,000 per second, and you can see the problem for using Bitcoin as a form of payment. Buying a cup of coffee at Starbucks with Bitcoin could potentially take an hour or longer just for the transaction to be processed. Not only this, the long wait time and number of "blocks" in the blockchain result in large fees when paying with Bitcoin. These two problems result in limited user adoption, however a solution has been proposed.

Many people love Bitcoin and want to see it succeed. As such, they are constantly coming up with solutions to make it better, and one such is the Lightning Network (LN). This network operates on top of the blockchain, essentially solving all the problems that plagued Bitcoin as a payment method. The LN has the capability to process millions of transactions a second, thus blowing away the capacity of even major credit card companies. Not only this, fees on the LN will be extremely low, or possibly even non-existent. Considering this, businesses may be more aptitude to accept Bitcoin, as they won't need to pay the 2%-4% charged by major credit cards companies. Thus they will be able to lower their prices for consumers, who will in turn pay with Bitcoin. It will become a perpetual motion machine.

The LN is still not in full capacity, but is likely to be slowly implemented in the near future. Once this occurs, you can rest assured that many more businesses will begin to accept Bitcoin, and user adoption will increase.

Bitcoin Halving

In order for new Bitcoins to be made, they have to be mined. Mining is an electricity intensive process which involves using a computer to solve complex mathematical equations. Once enough equations are solved, the miner receives a "block reward." When Bitcoin started, the block reward was 50 BTC. Every time 210,000 Bitcoin have been mined, the "block reward" is cut in half. At the time of writing this book, the current block reward is 12.5 BTC. The next expected halving is expected to take place in May 2020. This halving is a good thing. It keeps a finite amount of currency in circulation, and slowly trickles less and less out, thus reducing any sort of inflation that could be caused from too much Bitcoin in circulation at one time. It's like a cap on the amount of currency that can be printed, something the government likes to do the opposite of.

The first time this halving occurred was in 2012, in which the price of Bitcoin shot to an all-time high (at the time) of $1,000. Then, a second halving occurred in 2016, at which point Bitcoin shot up in price to its all-time high of $20,000; the next halving will be no different. As such, getting into Bitcoin before May 2020 will most likely be very beneficial.

The reasons for this increase in price is Economics 101: Supply & Demand. There is less Bitcoin available which equates to less supply. When there is less supply of something valuable, it goes up in price. It's the same with diamonds, gold, silver, etc. Think about gold mined here on earth. As more gold is mined in the earth, less is available to find and because of this, the price of gold increases. It's the same here with Bitcoin. As the value of a mining reward is cut in half, less Bitcoin is available to mine and as a result, the price increases.

Store of Value

Bitcoin is becoming the new gold. It is becoming a store of value that will continuously increase with time. Why is that? Well, unlike a governmental currency which can inflate, or hyperinflate in some cases, inflation cannot occur with Bitcoin.

This is because when Bitcoin was created, it was decided that there could be a total of 21 million in existence ever. As in, unlike governmental currency which can be printed at whim, no more Bitcoins can ever be made. This means inflation will never occur with Bitcoin and, once a stable currency, the price of it will only go up with time. This is a major separating factor of Bitcoin from common currency, and what is so enticing about it as a currency. If you put money under your mattress, it loses value. This forces people to put their money into stocks, savings accounts, etc. However with Bitcoin, you will be able to just hold it, and this "decrease in value" won't happen. It will be what the US dollar was pre-1913, before the establishment of The Federal Reserve.

Many times during recessionary periods and market crashes, people put their money in gold. The reason is because it is considered a "safe haven," and if sometime of collapse were to happen to the economy, fiat currency may not be safe. We are in the 11th year of a bull market in the United States, and a crash is likely to occur in the near future. Considering Bitcoin is becoming the new gold, I can say with near certainty that when a crash does occur, it will be a huge catalyst for Bitcoin. Instead of gold, many institutions and individual investors will put their money into Bitcoin, driving the price much higher.

Gold has a total world value, or *market cap*, of $6 trillion. Bitcoin is currently sitting around $300 billion. Considering this, strictly from a store of value standpoint, Bitcoin has the potential to increase 20x its value if it replaces gold. But unlike gold, it will not strictly be used as a store of value, but also a currency. This means its potential is even higher as it will be held by more people! Are you starting to see the reasons Bitcoin can increase so much?

Security

Bitcoin is more secure than cash. If you have a wallet with $500 US dollars (USD) in it, someone can steal that money from you, you can lose your wallet, etc. This can't happen with Bitcoin. Phones are password, fingerprint, and face ID protected. No one is getting into your Bitcoin account except for you.

Universal Currency

If you have a relative or friend in another country and want to send them money, you have to use services like Western Union, which cost money. There are other services, but all involve taking your currency and converting it into the currency of the recipient, and they all charge a fee to do this. Bitcoin is different. If your friend or relative has an app on their phone which holds Bitcoin, you can easily transfer them Bitcoin for free. No currency conversion, no charges, plain and simple.

Then we have international travelers. If you go outside of your country, you are forced to convert any cash you have into the domestic currency. This is time consuming, and exchange rates change constantly, meaning everyone has to keep up with current rates. But what if the vendors in the country you are traveling to accept Bitcoin? No more converting! Just whip out your phone, and pay with Bitcoin like you would in your home country. This makes Bitcoin a universal currency which can be used around the world.

No Taxes

While this feature may change, as greedy governments love taking every tax dollar they can get their hands on, currently Bitcoin is not taxed. The reason for this is because there is currently no way for third parties to identify, track, or intercept purchases made in Bitcoin. As such, sales tax is not added to purchases made in Bitcoin. If this continues, many people may move to paying in Bitcoin to avoid sales tax, which can be as high as 9.47% in some US states.

User Adoption

I think the main reason Bitcoin is still not widely accepted is because it has small amount of user adoption. Most people still use governmental currency to pay for items. However, I think this will soon change and this widespread user adoption is what will ultimately shoot Bitcoin through the ceiling.

At the beginning of Bitcoin mania, there was only a few not so reputable websites in which you could buy Bitcoin. They were rife with controversy and not considered very safe, with one example being Mt. Gox. This was a Japanese based Bitcoin exchange which was hacked in 2011 and taken for over 750,000 Bitcoins. This incident, as well as others like it, scared many from getting anywhere near Bitcoin. However, times have changed. There are now a plethora of apps which allow you to buy and sell Bitcoin, and safety has been taken in consideration. Scandals like Mt. Gox have forced Bitcoin exchanges to become safer, and hacking is much less of a problem now, especially with security features like two-factor identification. This means users won't need to fear their Bitcoin vanishing from their account, and many more people will start incorporating Bitcoin into their repertoire of payment methods.

There are also a few apps already released, with many more to come in the future, that allow you to spend Bitcoin right from your phone. Apps like SPEDN and BitPay have these features. Meaning you can walk into a retailer which accepts Bitcoin, scan your phone, and pay for your purchases with Bitcoin.

With apps like these, large companies are starting to accept Bitcoin in an increasing fashion. Look on the news and you'll see websites like NewEgg.com and Overstock.com accepting Bitcoin. Even large retailers like Home Depot and Whole Foods are now accepting Bitcoin payments in their store. These are just a few examples, and there are many more companies who are currently or will soon be accepting Bitcoin as payment in their stores.

While companies accepting Bitcoin doesn't automatically mean user adoption of Bitcoin, it definitely has some correlation. It's only a matter of time before a big fish like Amazon starts accepting Bitcoin and users will start thinking to themselves, "I wonder why Amazon accepts Bitcoin? Maybe I should try it out?" And at that time is when the Bitcoin rocket ship will greatly accelerate, as users will see the value Bitcoin has to offer.

WHY BITCOIN IS HERE TO STAY & HOW TO CAPITALIZE ON IT

◆ ◆ ◆

Won't Bitcoin Crash Again?

I admit it, when Bitcoin was going through its explosionary growth in late 2017 I thought it was a fad. Many compared it to Tulip Mania, a movement in Europe in the 1600's when the price of Tulips rose exponentially, and then quickly came crashing down. And as it went from its highs of $20,000 USD all the way down to $3,000 in late 2018, many were patting themselves on the back for not being sucked into the scam. But then something happened... it stopped going down. It maintained a bottom around $3,500 for a few months and slowly started moving higher... and then higher... and then higher. What this bottom and subsequent movement higher shows is Bitcoin is not gone, but is actually gaining traction again. And based on the information presented in this book, this traction will most likely stick, and stick for the long run.

People have been saying Bitcoin is "just a bubble," and was going to crash at $10, and $100, and $1,000, and $10,000. Bitcoin is currently in its 20th "bubble." And while it did move down in grand fashion from its high of $20,000 to around $3,000, when looked at on a "logarithmic" chart, it didn't actually "crash." You see, most charts that show Bitcoin are linear charts. If something priced at $1 increases to $2, it has moved up 100%. And if something priced at $10,000 increases to $20,000, it has moved up 100%. Logarithmic charts show a change based on percentage, where as linear charts show change based on dollar increments.

A $1 to $2 move looks much smaller in comparison to a $10,000 to $20,000 move on a linear chart, but in actuality they are the same percentage change. Let's first look at a typical chart of Bitcoin, as in a classic linear chart.

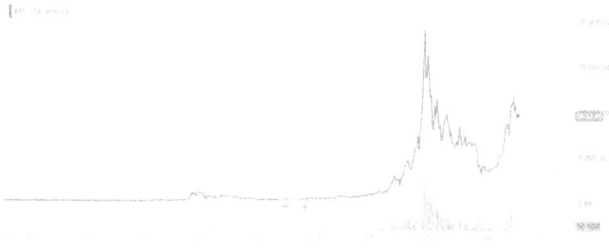

Looking strictly at this chart, it appears Bitcoin crashed in 2018, and is on its last limb. Now we will look at a more accurate logarithmic chart, showing strictly percentage changes over the same time period.

As you can see, while turbulent, Bitcoin never really "crashed," and has actually been steadily increasing over the years. And if the same trend continues, it will continue to increase in a similar fashion.

How to Capitalize on the Bitcoin Movement

At the time of writing this book, Bitcoin is currently hovering around $11,000. Many analysts are claiming within 1-2 years, Bitcoin will be valued at $100,000 US dollars (fastlink.xyz/bit1), and some even speculating it will go as high as 1 million US dollars by 2020 (fastlink.xyz/bit2). While I can't guarantee anything, I can say that I'm fairly confident Bitcoin will rise swiftly in the coming years, and we are lucky to still be in Bitcoin's infancy. As such, now is the time to get in on the action and capitalize before missing out on the explosive growth it will soon go through. So how can you do this?

While Robinhood started as a commission-free stock broker, they have expanded to allow users to buy into cryptocurrency. This means with Robinhood, you can buy into Bitcoin with no fees whatsoever. While you don't actually own a Bitcoin, you own a "stake" in it. Meaning your account balance, which is in US dollars, goes up or down based on the current market price of Bitcoin. At the time of producing this book, one Bitcoin is priced at around $11,000 USD. The beauty of Robinhood is they allow you to buy Bitcoin in any denomination you choose. As in if you want to buy .001 of a Bitcoin for $11, you can! With a modest price target of $100,000 USD in a few years, investing just $1,000 today would rise to almost $10,000 in a short period of time. And if Bitcoin does end up shooting up to $1,000,000, that $1,000 is now at almost $100,000!

Because Robinhood is so easy to use and user friendly, it is how I currently invest in Bitcoin. They have a great promotion going on where if you use the following link below, you get a free stock **valued up to $200** just for signing up! **It's completely free to sign up** and there are no fees to buy Bitcoin. And let's say the free stock you receive is worth $50. You can immediately sell the stock, and put that $50 into Bitcoin!

INTRODUCTION TO MAKE MONEY, LITERALLY... TODAY!

W hether you have $5.00 to invest or $5000, the one market you might consider investing your money in is cryptocurrency. Unless you are in the financial markets or a millennial who had discovered the bitcoin early on, cryptocurrency may sound like another fly by night scheme. But cryptocurrency is the past, present and future! Do not miss out!

This incredible method of investment is the new way to wealth and this book, Making Money in Cryptocurrency Today is going to show you how to get there! Let's give this financial buzz a closer look. You could spend hours upon hours researching for yourself on the Web to figure all this out…or you can read beyond these first few paragraphs and save yourself time AND money! And to most of us, time is money!

Some people believe if they did not get into bitcoin right away the chances for fortune and financial growth have passed them by. This is not true! Bitcoin is still growing! By the end of January, bitcoin is projected by some to reach $50,000 and those same enthusiasts believe bitcoin may reach 1 million by the end of 2021! It is not too late to buy portions of bitcoin!

And there are other forms of cryptocurrency as well. One spinoff of bitcoin has doubled in 10 days! No one expected that to happen! But I can tell you for sure, investors in cryptocurrency are going crazy this month trying to figure out what might be next! And we will show you how to find out as well! Within the pages of this book, you will learn just where various forms of cryptocurrency are now in value and possibly where they may go!

And while this book is not designed to guide you to invest or to advise you to invest, we will give you tons of education about the cryptocurrency form of investing. You will have questions and hopefully we will be help you find the answers!

This book was written to roll all your questions and answers into one place and help you make money in the crypto market right now... today! There is even one exchange site that is offering a small portion of bitcoin to use their site. They guide you through a few simple steps and then place the portion of bitcoin right in your wallet!

We will give you the instructions to help you go to this exchange if this is something you want to do in a later chapter. There are so many facets of bitcoin that are easy and other things about bitcoin that need extra effort before you invest.

We will have to get into the education of Cryptocurrency but you would not want your intelligence insulted by a get rich quick scheme. Cryptocurrency is for the intelligent investor! What this book does for you is to make the data and the terms on the crypto market easier to understand! And you can get everything you need to start investing within the short chapters of this easy read!

For starters, cryptocurrency is the only financial market that is open 24/7. This means you are able to buy or sale on your timetable. You do not have to wait for the bells of the stock market to ring or for the stockbrokers to answer their phones. Bankers hours are a thing of the past.

You are also able to learn at your own pace. You can read and reread pages of this book. Read a little and log into the investment exchange of your choosing and begin. Refer back to this resource for questions you might have again later. Even a beginner at investments is able to invest the minimum of a very few dollars to make the new fortune! Try that in the New York Stock exchange!

Again, the goal of this book is to shorten your research from going to multiple articles on the internet so that you only need this one book! Although there are many learning opportunities on the web for beginners and novices alike, this book will help solve your questions and give information for both experienced, and those who are just learning the terms of cryptocurrency. Why search anywhere else?!

Amazing Returns

The returns of Cryptocurrency far exceed those in the stock market, but alas, at times so do the risks. A big advantage of cryptocurrency is that YOUR money is YOUR money. You do not have to depend on where someone else who has invested for you places your funds, or what firm has ties to which stocks. YOU choose! YOU decide!

With cryptocurrency, the third party between exchanges is taken out of the equation. Every exchange is transparent and the exchange is from person to person. There is no need for a broker, bank, or any other person or entity who needs to make their share of whatever profits are involved.

In 2020, we have seen a fluctuation up and down in the markets. But Cryptocurrency has continued to gain and produce profits for investors. Some predict that Crypto will be a means of exchange in the future. Even PayPal has gotten into the act to help users easily invest. No matter your age, join the growing number of crypto investors in this New Era of wealth as you watch your money GROW!

Remember the cartoon, The Jetsons? They had Rosie the robot, moving exercise belts, refrigerators that could talk, computers, flying cars? Well, you get the idea. In many ways we have passed the Jetsons. While we do not have flying cars, our computer technology is far beyond anything the writers of the Jetson cartoon could imagine. We now hold in our hands a computer more powerful than the screen that George and Jane used to talk to each other during the day.

I do not recall the electronic exchange of funds in any futuristic shows of those space aged thematic shows, but I also never saw anything in the way of paper money either. Perhaps a barter system of trade was present because the authors did not quite know what to do with the idea of money. But the unspoken and understood concept was that actual paper money was and is antiquated.

After using debit/credit, PayPal, Venmo, Apple pay, and others, it only makes sense that people who have invested in bitcoin are starting to pay and shop using bitcoin. All of these methods are digital and virtual. There is no exchange of cash or check. The exchange of funds is from one person or business account to another. However, with a cryptocurrency such as bitcoin, there are no banks involved to guarantee the transaction. The transaction is verified and recorded on the blockchain.

As cryptocurrency, bitcoin was the first breakthrough cryptocurrency to get everyone's attention. For example, if you had invested just $10 US dollars in 2011 in bitcoin, and then did not sell when the value grew to $38 in 2013, you would have seen the money grow to over 2 million dollars by the end of 2020.

These stories will repeat throughout this book because bitcoin is phenomenal! It went through many ups and downs before soaring into the stratosphere of where it is now, but bitcoin is remaining consistently high and people can still buy portions of bitcoin. YOU CAN STILL BUY PORTIONS OF BITCOIN! And other coins, such as Ethereum, continue to rise in value as well!

We will help you education yourself so you can decide how to handle this information. You may want to jump on the cryptocurrency investment train after reading this book or you may say, "This is too risky. No thanks." Whichever the case, you will be able to make a decision with full knowledge of cryptocurrency after you finish reading this entire resource.

What's Next?

In this book, you will be given a guided tour through the necessary terms of cryptocurrency. These will be the terms that will be used throughout the book as well as terms you will need for successful investment.

Investment is the name of the game and we are all here to increase the size of our wallets! Remember, you want to be fully prepared when you make your first crypto purchase. And we will help you feel confident enough to do that. Confidence is important when you make your first purchase in the crypto market. Information spells confidence. Confidence makes the investment even stronger.

The more informed you are, the more confident you will be about your money and what you are doing with your money. Being educated and informed will make up for your lack of experience in cryptocurrency. And experience will come quickly once you read the information we are providing within these pages!

If you are an experienced crypto investor, we will confirm what you know and give you more tools for your cryptocurrency toolbox for investment. Again, the more you know, the more money you should make!

Do we make guarantees of profit? Of course not! That would be foolish! But we do guarantee you will not go into cryptocurrency blindly. You will learn from this book and you will not have to hunt and search all over the Internet to find what you want to know about Cryptocurrency.

Any investor must be informed of advantages and disadvantages. While there isn't a sure way to predict which cryptocurrency is going to be the next rising star, there are trends and we will discuss those with you.

The important idea about cryptocurrency is that it's still a fairly new currency but not so new that it's not on solid ground. In this case the solid ground is the blockchain and the community that supports it. So, you can still get in on the ground floor of investment! And we will show you how!

We will also take you into the community of how the Reddit cryptocurrency community shares back and forth. It is fun to watch the banter between others who invest and the fun they have together. It's a glimpse into the crypto investment world!

As stated previously, you can still buy bitcoin! Maybe not a whole bitcoin, but you can buy portions of bitcoin. We will also show you how to find other altcoins rising stars. Of course, you have to mind your money. One concept you will find from our book is that you have to do your own due diligence when investing.

Investing and the idea of trading is exciting! And, with this new book, you are going to share in this new excitement with us. Abundance awaits as you learn about cryptocurrency between the pages of our book. We will teach you the ins and outs of this important tool of exchange.

This Book is a Guide

Most importantly, we will guide you through how to obtain cryptocurrency and where to store your purchases. Remember, there is a guide of how to obtain a free portion of a bitcoin in Chapter 2! Our book is also going to give you information about the blockchain and how the blockchain works.

You will also get a brief history of cryptocurrency. History may or may not sound exciting to you, but we learn from what has happened. This is how we understand financial trends in the market. A smart investor learns from what has happened. And let's face it. Cryptocurrency's history isn't that long. It's a short history to learn!

As you learn about cryptocurrency and how to purchase, we will give you step by step instructions on how to create your wallet. This book will also let you know and repeat again and again how important it is to keep track of your wallet and your keys. You are going to understand the blockchain and how the blockchain is crucial to the purchase of cryptocurrency. The purchase, the blockchain, the keys and the wallet all go together and we will show you how this all works!

There are some people who may be interested in mining of bitcoin. The mining process will be completely discussed along with questions and answers that people have asked along the way about the mining process.

Finally, this book will present a fun facts and useful details some investors wish they had known before they invested even just a few years ago. Why not learn from the best investors before us?

You will find their advice helpful in order to your investment journey into cryptocurrency. Now is the time to begin making money, today!

OBTAINING CRYPTOCURRENCY AND YOUR WALLET!

This is the chapter you have been waiting for! How to get your hands on some Cryptocurrency for yourself! It's time to make some profit and you are ready! There are so many new investment currencies, and exchanges. We are going to show you the most user-friendly exchanges to help you begin a new way to finance your future!

We are going to look into the most user-friendly shopping sites and then you can make up your mind about where you want to purchase your first online currency. Investing is fun, user friendly and best of all, with our book, you can understand how to invest and get started immediately!

Coinbase

To begin, one of the most popular exchanges is Coinbase. And Coinbase is EASY! It is a highly recommended site for investing in bitcoin and altcoins. This is where you can obtain a FREE portion of bitcoin just for signing up.

In order to obtain your free portion of bitcoin, simply go to the Coinbase website: https://www.coinbase.com/join/5923adb56d1aff02e701806e. At the site you will be directed to sign up and create an account. Once you create an account, you will be directed to confirm your email and bank account.

The next step Coinbase asks you to do is upload your ID. This is not required, but if you upload your ID, (Some people do not wish to do this) you will receive a portion of bitcoin to add to your wallet. More about the "wallet" later.

Just like that, you own bitcoin! When you deposit $100 in your wallet using Coinbase, you get a bonus of $10. Coinbase does make every effort to become the most attractive investment exchange for newcomers to cryptocurrency.

CashApp

CashApp boasts that it is the best app for beginners as well. If you understand Venmo, you will understand CashApp because it works almost like Venmo. You are able to complete peer to peer transactions such as rent, splitting food, and a multitude of other uses as well as withdraw your bitcoin.

The interface is very easy which is why it is useful for beginners. One of the draw backs is that there is a 3% charge for every transaction. The site only uses bitcoin at this time. Withdraws are limited to $2000 of bitcoin within 24 hours.

Binance

This site is geared toward more advanced users in part because of the more advanced charting. There are 13 states where Binance is not available including New York.

This exchange began in 2017 and specializes in the altcoin. So, if altcoin is your jam, and you feel you have more experience, you might give this site a try or you may already be active on this site. Binance has more international trading pairs than in the US, but still has over 100 trading pairs in the United States.

How do I make My Purchase?

The next question is: How do I purchase cryptocurrency? To buy cryptocurrency of any kind, you need a wallet. The next section is going to tell you what a wallet is and how to create a wallet. This book is the one place where you will get all the needed information to become a cryptocurrency investor!

The Wallet

What is a cryptocurrency wallet? The wallet contains the public and private keys to pairs of public and private cryptographic keys. The keys can be used to track ownership, in order to receive or spendcryptocurrencies. A public key allows others to make payments to the address and a private key enables the spending of cryptocurrency from the address of the wallet owner.

If you lose your keys, in effect, you have lost your cryptocurrency. The keys stand for your currency and the value in the currency. If someone else has your keys, they have the coins. Your wallet is a virtual symbol, and in some cases can even be located on your phone.

You would never give someone the password to your bank account. Do not give people your keys to your wallet. If you have a multi-signature wallet, this is designed for more signatures on transactions and in many ways is more secure.

You can have absolute and complete control over your money! That's what this is all about. And to do that, you need your digital wallet. This is a vital step for all cryptocurrency investors. Opportunities and advantages are waiting for you!

To create a cryptocurrency wallet, follow the instructions below:

1. Go to myetherwallet.com
2. Once you are on the site, under the main menu, go to "New Wallet" so you can create a new wallet.
3. Now you will be asked for a password.
4. Type in your password and then click on "Create New Wallet."
5. Download your keystore/json file. Make sure you safely store both your password and your file.
6. You will then be led to your private key. This is vital information you should keep safe and never share.
7. Congratulations! You have created your wallet!

Now that you have your wallet you can use your account to purchase altcoins or bitcoins for investment. But hang on! You need to learn more about cryptocurrency before you start spending your money.

Where Should You Store Your Wallet?

It's so tempting to store your wallet on your phone or tablet where you can have very easy access. But that easy access is also a tempting target for the criminal element as well. Especially if you travel in and out of airports, or internationally.

The absolute saftest thing to do is to store your wallet on a USB stick to keep in a safe place to only use when you are working on your wallet and investments. Whatever the case, use a special device to store your wallet and cryptocurrency information so that you have to work to log on.

Lloyds of London does offer an insurance policy for your wallet if it is lost by theft. This is not if you lose your key, but if your wallet is somehow stolen. This will protect a wallet from as little as $1275 USD to a much higher amount. This insurance policy is also backed by the usual assortment of Lloyd's insurers, including Markel and TMK. This liability insurance will have a limit that will increase or decrease in line with the crypto assets in the individual wallets. An introductory price for wallets less than $10,000 USD is $29.00 and for larger amounts the price was just over $200.

What if I want to sell my cryptocurrency?

You've invested, made money but you have a feeling it's time to let your bitcoin or whatever currency you have go. What do you do? We have the steps to take you through the trade or selling your bitcoin or whatever you have to sell!

1. Go to the exchange site you use when you purchase cryptocurrency.
2. Hit the trade button
3. Select "Sell"
4. Select the currency you desire to sell and direct it to sell off of your fiat wallet
5. After that, choose your wallet and select withdraw.

There is a short waiting period until your funds are available. During that time, any increase or decrease in the cryptocurrency value will not affect your funds after your sell. Your exchange will alert you when your funds are ready for a transfer into your bank account.

ADVANTAGES AND DISADVANTAGES OF CRYPTOCURRENCY

Think back to when you were 12 years old. What would you do if your grandma gave you $1000? Well, in 2011 a boy named Erik Finman received $1000 from his grandma for his 12th birthday and that little guy invested his money in, you guessed it, bitcoin! He was able to buy two.

However, when it grew to $1200 each, he sold them. Still thinking of investment, he bought a video education company called Botangle. This was a video company that did some kind of online tutoring services. Not long after the company grew and investors wanted to buy the company for $100,000 or 300 bitcoin.3

As you probably guessed again, Erik took 300 bitcoin. Now, the story doesn't say anything about his parents, but I'm guessing, they were fairly savvy as well. Long story short, Erik became a millionaire off of that 300 bitcoin in not too long of a time! What a smart kid!

To be on the ground floor of bitcoin is woulda, coulda, shoulda. But bitcoin is still there. And investors are still predicting bitcoin may stabilize and become a currency similar to the US dollar or the Euro. If that happens the investment opportunity is still promising to be profitable and wild!

There are still many altcoins as well to invest in. No one can be sure which altcoin could be the next coin to go exponentially! If a twelve-year old kid can figure this out, you can too!

So, let's talk about some advantages and disadvantages.

Advantages

- Inflation Does Not Affect Cryptocurrency – Cryptocurrency is insulated against inflation. When demand increases, so does value. This in turn keeps up with the market sand then the value in the long run protects the currency from inflation.
- Cryptocurrency is decentralized. Even though

someone had to create the currency, no one person or organization can control what happens with the currency once it has been released for purchased.

- Transactions are faster than transactions through banks. Verification takes seconds and even international transactions can happen instantaneously.
- Governing and maintaining of any cryptocurrency is accurate and keeps the integrity of the currency. Miners are paid to do their job (more in chapter 5) so they keep all transactions up to date and logged accurately.
- The blockchain assures that all transactions are secure and private. Every transaction is on the blockchain with a unique code. Only the users with the unique profile have the keys to understand the transactions.
- Currency exchanges are completed easily. The Euro can be switched to the US dollar and so on by trading in cryptocurrency. This is another way to use currency in your wallet.
- You might just make a ton of money! It's happened to many before you and it just happened to some one today! Be brave and see how this goes! Experts agree that $100 can take you a long way to start your investment into the Crypto Generation!
- It's fun if you have the money to invest! Watching the money grow and becoming involved in this investment community is fun and interesting!
- Cryptocurrency might just be the economy of the future and you have the chance to get in on the ground floor! What better advantage is there?

Disadvantages

- If you lose data, you can have financial loss. Cryptocurrencies are safe unless you lose your keys. In reality, cryptocurrency is completely safe, but the loss of a key will in effect, lock up your wallet, making it impossible to get your currency.
- Mining has an adverse effect on the environment. Not like you might imagine, but indirectly, yes. The mining takes a large amount of computer energy. People are on the computer for hours and days trying to mine bitcoin, especially. The miners in China are using electricity and therefore using a large amount of coal to stay on the grid. The energy footprint on our environment is tremendous.
- What if you send funds to the incorrect destination? The wrong wallet? Oh, too bad, so sad. And this is also one of the ways that people can be cheated out of funds. When a wallet is set up and then it is used to create purchases dishonestly. Where the buyer then does not get their product.
- Cryptocurrencies can be used for illegal transactions. Personal wallets are very hard to trace by the government, so transactions are likewise hard to trace, legal or illegal.
- You might lose money. That part is not fun.

UNDERSTANDING THE BLOCKCHAIN

I f you are a computer science geek you have known about the term blockchain for years, but for those of us who are not as computer aware, we need to learn about the block chain to truly understand cryptocurrency investing and how the process works.

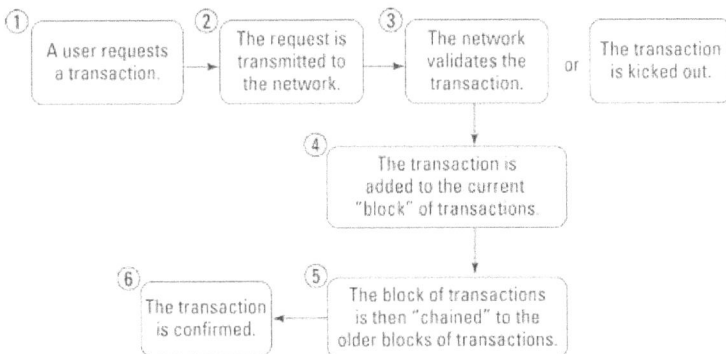

① A user requests a transaction. → ② The request is transmitted to the network. → ③ The network validates the transaction. or The transaction is kicked out.

④ The transaction is added to the current "block" of transactions.

⑥ The transaction is confirmed. ← ⑤ The block of transactions is then "chained" to the older blocks of transactions.

How blockchains work.

When we discussed the terms, we mentioned that the blockchain was much like it said, blocks on a chain. Below is an example of a simple transaction of a cryptocurrency transaction on a blockchain. By looking at the diagram, the blockchain becomes much easier to understand.

BLOCKCHAINS RECORD the data of all the transactions. And once a transaction is complete, it is very difficult to erase the transaction data. Therefore, a blockchain becomes a permanent record of the history of the transactions as long as the network stays permanent. And this depends on the community that supports the network.

The three types of blockchains are private blockchains, public blockchains, and permissioned blockchains.

- Public blockchains are what they say, public. They are open for anyone to use. Bitcoin is on a large distribution network and is public. These blockchains are always an open source. Their community maintains they stay open. We will discuss the importance of cryptocurrency community in the next chapter.
- Private blockchains are much smaller and they tend to have a group of trusted members that trade confidential information.
- Permissioned blockchains control the different roles that each individual plays within the network. These blockchains tend to be larger and the core code might be private or open.

Blockchain's Impact on Society

There are many contributions to society that blockchain has had direct impact. Cryptocurrency and the blockchain have changed the way we trust transactions. Because transactions are made at lightening speed, there is no room for even a minor gap between these transactions.

1. Peer to peer organizations such as Airbnb and Uber are assisted on their apps by the blockchain because it can create a decentralized network for them to operate business.
2. In community service, blockchain is being studied by civic organizations to help combat election fraud.
3. Blockchain is also being used by a number of area services to transfer data over the web in order to assist with traffic management, trash collection, and transportation.
4. In this trying time of healthcare, blockchain has also done its part to help send and store confidential patient information and data to the appropriate authorized providers.

Blockchain has only continued to grow in value and usefulness. Please be clear. An individual cannot purchase blockchain, but rather use blockchain as a means of transferring funds and making purchases of bitcoin and altcoin.

There are ways to invest in the blockchain.

- **Stockpiling bitcoin** is the number one way to invest in the blockchain. As we now know, bitcoin is very expensive even for a small share. But if bitcoin grows, even a small share will prove to be a solid investment.
- **Penny stocks** are another way to invest in the blockchain. Cryptocurrency has penny stocks. But just like anything else, watch your pennies. We can compare penny stocks to a penny slot machine. Pennies add up to dollars really fast. Don't spend more pennies than you can lose. Be aware that some

of the altcoins that cost mere pennies are junk. You
will lose all of your money on junk.

- **Crowdfunding** is the third way we are going to
  mention in this chapter to invest in the blockchain.
  This method uses altcoins. The total supply of coins is
  mined and then sold in an initial coin offering. One
  coin network that used this method to get started was
  Bitshares. This is a good way to get into a ground floor
  of a coin and a new network.

When a business makes a transaction that is just a regular
transaction, of course it keeps records of the transaction. Now,
on the computer, but some individuals still do a backup paper
ledger, just in case. These transactions take up time and space.

Not only are these transactions costly in human hours, they
may also be prone to human error. And human errors can cost
thousands and more dollars to investors. In the new system that
we now call the blockchain system, the computer records or the
ledger is replaced by a larger network.

This network is made up of identical databases. Every
change that occurs is recorded on the blockchain as a permanent
record. And the third party is eliminated. Instead of the transactions taking time and space, these transactions happen instantaneously.

The less time between transactions, the less time there is for
any type of error. Blockchain transactions take nanoseconds and
are without human intervention. The blockchain has literally
helped to speed up and make all online transactions seamless
and cryptocurrency transactions within less than a second.

COMMUNITY AND CONFIDENCE OF INVESTMENT

W hat is the significance of community in cryptocurrency? What is the significance of community to anyone either online or in daily life? Our daily lives revolve around community. Community is essential. In cryptocurrency, community is also essential. People must have a forum to be able to come together in order to discuss challenges and interests with people from all over the world.

Being able to have an online community to support the cryptocurrency and the people involved in transactions is vital to the altcoin or bitcoin. The community enables users to have easier access to clients and to other people with which they want to communicate.

When a community is committed, then the motivation to move forward is high. Having a successful community directly relates to a successful product. These communities used to be live events when a currency was born, but because of coronavirus, the communities form online. And the online communities are active and going 24/7 just like the currencies. You literally can reach out any time day or night and find someone in your currency community or the cryptocurrency in general and find someone of like mind with which to cuss and discuss.

Usually, members of each community are involved, meaning they are direct investors, writers, developers, analysts, and others. These people have the most to gain and the most to lose.

Reddit and Cryptocurrency

Reddit is also a cryptocurrency community of sorts. There is one section of Reddit that is creative and just plain fun. The people who post support each other through ups and downs of crypto investing. And they don't hesitate to poke fun at themselves!

Going to Reddit to watch the discussion on cryptocurrency is a fun time. This is for new and experienced investors alike! There are a lot of inside jokes such as "Bitcoin is down to $2.70 a pop. So glad I didn't buy into that mess!" It's incredibly fun as we take a laugh at ourselves!

Please know Reddit is all opinion. It's a group of people just sharing what they know or what they *think* they know. There are no sure answers on Reddit. Only discussion and fun. But if you want some fun about cryptocurrency, go to Reddit and enjoy. The memes are hilarious as well! Be aware there will be advertising trying to take advantage of rookies!

One particularly funny little blurb:

"My 64 year old dad's analysis of why I should not invest in cryptocurrency:

'You know, the Russians are eventually going to hack the four-chain through a back door that nobody knows about.'

I immediately went home to put another $500 in in various cryptocurrencies. The only thing he proved to me is that when his generation dies off, this shit is going to skyrocket!'

And there are also life stories such as this 27 year old shared:

"I sold out my remaining crypto last night. Still feels surreal to me. Started buying Ethereum at just above $2 in early 2016 after missing the boat on Bitcoin. I put my whole tax return in in 2016 and threw a couple hundred at it whenever I could. I didn't buy a car and biked to work to save money. I remember at the time thinking there was about a 1/3 chance it would 100x, so there was an asymmetrical risk/reward in my opinion.

Sold a large chunk during the previous bull run in 2017 and sold the remaining in multiple sales this January. Averaged about a 150x on my cost basis across all sales. All long-term capital gains. Now I'm 27 and financially independent. Will be buying my parents a house this year.

I love this community and hope both the technology and price will continue to improve. Thanks to everyone for making this a fun ride!"

That was a letter of report from someone who definitely was active on Reddit and appreciated the crypto community and the community he had on Reddit. The fun and the money he made were definitely appreciated. He was one of the lucky ones! And it does take luck. He also did not just sit back. He made changes and sold crypto along the way and moved from one coin to another. That takes experience, research, and know how.

Confidence

The investors we talked to who had experience gave us some ideas as to what they wish they had known or read about prior to investing in cryptocurrency. This is what we to bring to you so that you are able to invest with more confidence than even the more experienced investor had when they began!

1. Have a strategy. Don't just invest willy nilly. Know when and why you are getting into a currency and have an exit plan.
2. Invest small. One investor invested twice with $100 and both times cashed out at $5000. He either had a plan or was extremely lucky. Whichever the case, and probably the latter, he knew when to exit. Invest small unless you have a large amount to invest and then shoot the wad. You could make a killing!
3. Do tons of research. Which is what this book is about. Is research always entertaining? Well, we've tried to make this book as fun as possible, but sometimes you just have to learn the facts. Now it's up to you to research the different coins and numbers and see which ones seem to be growing and which you want to invest time and money.
4. Always invest on the blockchain. If a cryptocurrency isn't on the blockchain as of yet, don't do There are over 5000 altcoins that you might think, "Hey I'm going to get on the ground floor of this new coin."

There are tons of coins that are just a waste of money.
They are pure junk and will sink down to zero and
you will lose every cent you invested.

5. Are you a long-term trader or someone who wants to
   invest and get out? Decide which type of trader you
   want to be and then do not let anyone throw you off
   your game.

Learn from the experiences of people who have been active
in cryptocurrency before you and from those who are investing
currently. These are the people who help make up the community. And remember, while this book is about investing, we in no
way advise anyone in any way to invest in any form of cryptocurrency.

Confidence in cryptocurrency is rising. Compared to even 10
years ago, people thought it was laughable to put money in
cryptocurrency. Maybe some even thought it might be a joke.
But now there are many who have more confidence in say, the
bitcoin than they do often used currency.

In places around the globe where there are no banking
systems, cryptocurrency is being used now as the preferred
system where the nearest bank is miles away. Confidence in
crypto is growing in developing countries faster than antici-
pated, but the reasons make perfect sense.

Baby boomers also are joining the Crypto Generation as they
look for ways to make sure their investments are diversified.
And the very young are getting involved as gamers. About one
third of the world's population considers themselves to be
gamers.6

With the rise of blockchain gaming, many gamers reap bene-
fits of Non-fundable Tokens. NFT. People can pay extra money
to unlock levels on games such as Fortnite and World of
Warcraft. They are using the blockchain and do not even realize
they are funding cryptocurrencies.

You know confidence is growing because conversations are growing as well. More and more you will hear of people asking questions about investing and also just wanting to know what cryptocurrency is. You are ahead of the average person on the street because you have this book!

Why the buzz around Ethereum?

Some investors will tell you that Ethereum is the next cryptocurrency to go viral. And some will say it already has! The latest news shows that in the first few days of 2021 the price of Ethereum has increased 60%. You would say confidence is very high. This is the world's 2nd largest cryptocurrency. And usually when bitcoin rises, investors in bitcoin start to diversify and this is why Ether is picking up speed as well. For example, Ether has gone from $750 at the beginning of January to $1400 on January 19, 2021. Bitcoin also rose $29,000 to $35,000 in that same time period.

Remember though, these coins can come and go. Ripple, the 3rd largest coin just hit bottom because of a lawsuit. So, everyone who had money in Ripple, lost all of their money that they had in this altcoin. This market is full of spikes and drops and because the market is open 24/7 anything can happen at any time. Keep that in mind should you decide to invest.

MINING

So, you do not what to buy cryptocurrency, but you would rather mine the coins. Are you a techno expert? Please realize, a regular home computer is not fully functional to mine bitcoin. There are other ways to do this, so please read further.

In the Bitcoin network, miners try to add blocks when they mine, to the blockchain, by solving various mathematical problems. This requires enormous computational and electrical power. While many miners compete to add each block, the miner who solves the problem will actually add the block—along with its approved transactions—to the blockchain. This miner receives a reward of 6.25 bitcoins (as of January 2021). 6

Can you Make Money Mining?

Let's examine what bitcoin is worth and what it takes to mine. One bitcoin is worth $18,000 and the miner who gets the block on the chain gets 6.25 coins. That is a sum total of $112,500. Seemingly, that's a tidy sum. Now let's examine the cost involved.

The specialized mining hardware for mining called application-specific integrated circuits, or ASICs may cost between $100 to $10,000. This cost is only a fraction of what the expense is to run the software. The electricity needed to run this program is somewhere close to the same amount of running 500 PlayStation 3 devices.

But do not despair if you have the brain that is geared toward this type of technology. You can join a pool with other people. This will save on cost of electricity and other expenses. There are several well-known pools including F2Pool, Poolin, and BTC.com.

To get started mining:

- Calculate your cost and your possible profit. You know investment profit can go up or down. The cost is easier to figure. You can research and figure out pretty closely what mining is going to cost you.
- Join a pool. This will help with your resources, but a pool will also cut into your profits. When a mining pool makes money, the whole pool shares in the

profits, but sometimes the funds do not show up until 1200 days later.

- Get the hardware needed. As stated above, your hardware is going to cost anywhere from several hundred dollars to several thousand to begin your mining project.
- Consult with other pool members. Other people who are in pools can be your best resources for help.
- Always do your research. Choose your mining software and choose the platform to access the blockchain.
- Remember to keep good records. You have to pay taxes on profits from mining. You will be taxed on the value of the bitcoin on the day it is mined.
- Install a bitcoin wallet. By now you have everything you need to create a wallet from chapter III.

Why is Cryptocurrency Important?

Cryptocurrency is important because people are using this form of currency all over the world. Several large banks, including Bank of America are using forms of cryptocurrency. Some financial institutions are creating and launching their own. J.P. Morgan is using Zcash. While not giving advice, this might not be a bad investment.

If you have extra money and you want to invest, then perhaps this is for you. If you like Las Vegas, this is somewhat like a casino. Cryptocurrency is a gamble, so do not invest money you cannot afford to lose. And have that plan we discussed. Know when to say when.

You need to know at what point you are going to say, "Ok, I've won enough and I'm ready to stop and sell." There is that point with cryptocurrency and you have to decide that point before you get started.

Just like on a Blackjack table. You might start out with $100 and say, "Ok, if I lose down to $30 in this session, I am out. And Likewise, if I win up to $300, I am also out. You have to make a plan with investments. You have a number to enter and a number to exit.

We've established that cryptocurrency is important but when did cryptocurrency start to matter?

Cryptocurrency has so much room to grow, but you also have to be very careful with your money. Investment is fun, especially if the currency grows and continues to grow, but make sure you are ready to cash out when the time is right or keep riding the wave if you see fit!

What gives a currency it's worth if just anyone can create a coin and try to market it? The simple reason is cryptocurrencies must be backed by a community and the collective community must believe in its worth. People ultimately decide what we value. What we consider to be of value, usually at some point becomes scarcer and the price rises as a result.

China – The Mining Capitol of the World

Inner Mongolia has become the place where mining has become the Bitcoin Capitol of the world! China, because of its cheap electricity, and low cost of resources, is the place where bitcoin mining hit a record high in June of 2019.

A large portion of bitcoin's network including Bitmain, F2Pool, and others are all located in China. This indicates the mining direction point toward this region for the most results and profits due to the low costs of the mining process.

Competition for mining in China has surprised the world and is located to the North from the Arctic Circle. Again, the resources are less expensive. The very cold temperatures are also attractive and the power supply is not linked to any Russian grid, so the cost is extremely low.

Customers in that area of the world pay the cheapest rates for electricity. One farm in the tundra hired locals who were trained by experts and this plant mines an average of 6 bitcoins per day. This is not even the main plant. The main plant does so well that individual miners earn 6.25 bitcoin for every block they mine. A block being about $90,000 in bitcoin.

New Development of Regulations

The United States Department Financial Crimes Enforcement Network (FinCIN) recently proposed new regulations for financial institutions that deal with cryptocurrencies such as bitcoin. Basically, when a buyer makes a purchase of currency over $10,000 exchanges will be required to file a report with FinCIN.

Anytime an exchange is made in a noncustodial wallet for greater than $3000, the report must also be made. Translated, this means, that if a person buys bitcoin for $3000 or more, and moves the coin to a wallet they own or control, they must have proof the wallet is theirs, by providing identification, address, and keys, of course.

For many cryptocurrency users this means very little, but for some, this will mean some irritation as bitcoin and altcoin purchases were usually somewhat free of red tape. And with new regulations, there are a few more hoops to jump through. Again, this is for larger money investors.

Other Important Cryptocurrencies

1. Litecoin began in 2011 and seemed to follow right behind bitcoin. Charles Lee created Litecoin and it was based on an open-sourced global payment. Litecoin is a lot like bitcoin but it faster in creation and faster in transaction. Litecoin is the 6th largest currency in the world and is a token value of $153.88 USD.

2. Ethereum is the coin that is actually in line second to bitcoin. Nowhere near in the same value range, but still promising growth. Ethereum has split into Ethereum (ETH) and Ethereum Classic (ETC). One token is valued at $1,218.59. USD.

3. Polkadot (DOT) is said by some to be the next Ethereum. At trading for $12.54 for a share in January 2021, this is an affordable investment with good predictions. Polkadot's blockchain has security and community so it appears to look more solid than years previously. It was created by Gavin Wood, who was also involved in Ethereum.

4. Stellar (XLM) is an open blockchain network. It helps provide enterprise solutions by connection financial for the action of larger transactions. Stellar was founded by Jed McCaleb, who originally came from Ripple Labs. Stellar trades for .27 USD.

5. Cardano (ADA) This cryptocurrency was created by mathematicians, engineers, and cryptography experts. This was co-funded by Charles Hoskinson, who also helped with Ethereum, after being disillusioned about the direction it was going. Although Cardano is in its early stages, this system has a goal to be the financial system of the world. Currently, it trades for $0.31 USD

6. Bitcoin Cash (BCH) This is one of the successful off shoots of the original Bitcoin. One of the first altcoin rise on the blockchain. Historically, when different factions of a cryptocurrency cannot agree, one will fork off and begin a new coin. It will have a new code. BCH began in August of 2017 because of one of these splits. Currently each token sells for $513.45 USD.

7. Tether is in a group of "stablecoins." This is a group of coins that try to smooth out the fluctuations often associated with cryptocurrency. Interestingly, Tether's price is tied to the US dollar. This makes this currency's transfer back and forth into and from dollars very quick and simple. At the current time, one token is worth $1.00 USD.

8. Binance Coin (BNB) originally operated on the

Ethereum blockchain and then had its own launch with its own exchange. The Binance exchange is one of the more widely used around the world. The current worth of BNB as of January 2021 is $44.26 USD per token.

9. Monero (XMR) is very private and untraceable which makes it very attractive to a certain crowd. The cryptography community latched on quickly in 2014 and this currency grew because of the community support. Because of the privacy and the ability to be completely untraceable, the currency has lent itself to have a more criminal interest around the world. Transactions are not easily tracked on any form of blockchain. Monero has a per token value of $158.37 USD.

10. Chainlink lays claim to many uses for it's system. Being involved in the monitoring of water supply, pollution control, flood warnings in various cities, as well as keeping data on water flow, a Chainlink oracle relays this information for the good of the communities it serves. Currently, one LINK is valued at $21.53 USD.

FUN FACTS AND FACTS YOU MUST KNOW

1. You Can Track Anyone's Cryptocurrency Wallet – Every transaction is traceable. If you have the name of the person, wallet address, wallet ID, you can find the transaction on the blockchain. This is transparency. This lowers incidents of fraud and

2. Bitcoin is not out of your reach! Even today you can purchase a portion of bitcoin. Just like we mentioned early in this book, Coinbase will give you a small

portion of bitcoin. Here's what you can buy in bitcoin for $1.00. You can buy 00014 bitcoin for $1.00 USD.

3. Even though we know the name of the creator of bitcoin is "Satoshi Nakamoto" that is not really his name. We do not know who this person is. There is actually some anonymous person behind bitcoin who we don't know who he is. And probably for good reason. He would have zero peace after his creation of bitcoin. As the rumor goes, he has billions of bitcoins.

4. Don't lose your wallet. If you lose your wallet, you've lost your investments and the money they represent. This isn't like losing a debit card. You can't get the wallet back. It's gone.

5. Cryptocurrency is extremely shaky. Some people use the word, volatile. Whatever word you choose the meaning is the same. The value can go either way at any given minute so be ready with your investment plan.

6. Vancouver, Canada, and Silicone Valley, California have bitcoin machines, just FYI!

7. You might be able to catch gossip on the Web on forums such as Reddit about which coins might do what. This is just gossip. Take it with a grain of salt. No one is advising you to act on gossip.

8. Bitcoin is limited resource just like other resources that cannot be replenished. As bitcoin is mined, and the resource is on the blockchain and used, the resource diminishes and therefore becomes more valuable. It's basic supply and demand economics. As the supply goes down the demand and value seem to keep going up.

9. As the demand for bitcoin continues to rise, so do the creation of altcoins. There are over 5000 altcoins. Admittedly some are junk. Watch out for those. Check

out the trends and how the coins perform over time. Don't just buy cryptocurrency because it is cheap. You are still spending your hard-earned money. Cryptocurrency is alive and also volatile!

10. The smallest unit of bitcoin is called a satoshi. The satoshi is a .00000001 of a bitcoin. When you buy small amounts of bitcoin you are buying Sats. For $1.00 USD you can buy about 43 Sats.

11. The famous money maker Warren Buffet thinks Bitcoin is just a bad joke.

12. There will only ever be 21 million bitcoins. Bitcoins actually have a limit. That's why people who mine, say cryptocurrency is a limited resource.

13. The honey badger is bitcoin's unofficial animal mascot??

14. Bitcoin mining consumes about as much energy as a midsized country. (About the size of Chili)

15. What world leaders say about cryptocurrency matters. When they make public statements, cryptocurrency activity can rise or fall according to the negativity or positivity of their statements.

16. Billionaire investor and trader Paul Tudor Jones declared bitcoin as his top guess for investing against post-pandemic inflation.

17. There are over 200 million wallets, but only about 40% of them are considered active. Does this mean the currency is lost? Does it mean the bitcoin or altcoin is just sitting in the wallet and forever will remain with no claim? These and other mysteries are definitely a challenge of our future!

18. There are seven countries that have banned cryptocurrency:

- Algeria

- Bolivia
- Ecuador
- Nepal
- Bangladesh
- Cambodia

1. Cryptojacking is a term used when thieves get ahold of your phone or computer and put a malicious code into your device in order to obtain your keys and your wallet. This is when you can lose your currency. How can you detect this has happened? Your phone or computer will become extremely slow or your battery will constantly be needing a charge, even when your phone/computer has not been used very long.
2. You can freeze your cryptocurrency asset on a flash drive or on a hard drive on your computer to protect it from theft.

Free Courses on Cryptocurrency

1. Coinbase Earn – This exciting course is a course where you actually earn small amounts of cryptocurrency after learning and answering questions about the topic. You will get a well-rounded view on altcoin and other than the standard coins you hear about more often.
2. Coinbase Learn – This site uses a set of flashcards to help you learn all the concepts about buying, selling, the blockchain, and mining. This is a great course to get up to speed fast.
3. 101 Blackboard Series – This course is a YouTube series to help with technical elements of bitcoin, private keys, and the blockchain. This also helps

investors understand the risks that are associated with cryptocurrencies.

4. Coursera (Bitcoin and Cryptocurrency Technologies) offered by Princeton University – This course will offer to you basic cryptography techniques and then will link them to the bitcoin. This is taught mainly through videos and has an emphasis on bitcoin security. A short amount of time is devoted to altcoins as well.

5. Ethereum (Learn Section) – This course will educate the user about Ethereum just like the title says. It is actually very impartial because it includes pluses and minuses of the currency. If you want to know more about Ethereum, this is the course for you!

Why are More Men Involved In Cryptocurrency?

The wave of cryptocurrency has in the past leaned heaving toward men. In fact, in 2018, men made up 91% of bitcoin purchases.4 But there are a group of women who are aiming to change that statistic and by 2020 they certainly have. Women of all ages and demographics now own bitcoin and various altcoins with historic gains of wealth and influence across the globe.

A large number of investment groups for women have sprung up in the United States. These groups are composed of moms, grandmothers, working class professionals, and women who travel across the world to connect with other investors, and meet on a regular basis with each other. These groups provide support, financial advice, and connection for the next level of investment on the internet.

A Chance to Rise Up From Poverty

Cryptocurrency is seen by some as a chance for immigrants who are new to a country to be able to have a banking system before becoming a citizen. Becoming a citizen takes time and resources. Many banks will not allow a person to open a bank account without proof of citizenship from the country they are currently living in.

These people are "unbanked." But with cryptocurrency, if they have a phone, they have a way of exchange of funds. Digital currency gives the person a chance to store and use funds without having to have a bank. This may help to get people out of poverty quicker.

India Ban Drives Cryptocurrency Underground

Because of a 2019 recommendation to ban cryptocurrency in India, you could be put in jail for up to 10 years for owning a cryptocurrency and living in India. The appeals and charges continue to go back and forth in India, so that the country does not have an "official" ban as of yet, but the risk is said not to be worth pushing the envelope.

Standing committees continue to revisit the bill to solidify this ban and in the meantime, the buying and selling of cryptocurrency in India has slid underground. The other serious impact is that India's largest exchange has relocated from India to Malta. Lawmakers in India argue the "The Constitution of India Article 19(1)(g) gives us the fundamental right of freedom to conduct business in any sector or trade."But the action in the courts could easily take up to five years. If India waits too long to give traders the green light, sadly, India will be the country that loses out on the investment opportunity.3

Can You Put Cryptocurrency in Your Will?

You've invested and your investments are growing nicely. But tomorrow, unknown to you, you are going to have a massive heart attack! What happens to your cryptocurrency and your wallet? Does someone you care about have the keys in your wallet and is that even legal?

One of the best things about cryptocurrency is that when you are alive, no one can get to it! But if you die, also, no one can get to it! For one thing, most Crypto exchanges do not allow you to name someone as the beneficiary if you die. And even the largest exchange, Coinbase, will not flag the assets. It is up to the family to come forward.

Coinbase Exchange will allow your chosen loved one to show a death certificate and access the wallet if they are the named beneficiary and you have given them the key codes needed to access the wallet. NO EXCHANGE IS GOING TO GIVE OUT THE SEQUENCE OF NUMBERS. Remember if you lose your keys at any given time, your investment is lost.

MAKE SURE SOMEONE KNOWS YOU HAVE CRYPTOCURRENCY.

You can leave who you want to have the cryptocurrency in a will. You should leave details of who currency goes to, but you cannot leave the keys to the wallet in the will because a will can become public record. Put something like the keys in a safety deposit box and make sure the person whom you want to have your crypto wallet also gets the key to your safety deposit box.

You could make a game of it, I guess and have people try and guess your keys with a series of clues. Whoever wins, wins your fortune! Do what you want, but make sure someone gets the currency. If your currency is sizable, of course you should have a person to whom knows your finances and hopefully knows where your keys are kept and is able to access your cryptocurrency.

Do you know how much has been lost due to death and lack of planning? Experts say over 3.7 million bitcoins are just gone. That's a net worth of about 24 billion dollars! Wasted. All because someone wasn't thinking about the future.

Lesson #234 make a plan for your cryptocurrency the day you invest in cryptocurrency! Tell your spouse, or grown children, or a trusted someone. Or, put instructions neatly in a message somewhere so you have it legally ready for the day when loved ones are surprised by your passing.

A Personal Story:

The following is a personal story of my cryptocurrency buy in. I decided to take $100 and buy Ethereum, Chainlink, a portion of bitcoin, and Cardano. I have kept the currency during the writing of this book. Before I took my $100, I had to ask myself, "If what I buy drops to zero the very next week, am I prepared to say goodbye to my $100?"

Now, anyone who knows me knows I do not like to gamble with my money, but after doing the research for this book, I was convinced to try at least $100 and see what happens. After all, if you write nonfiction, you should your material firsthand or have really done your research. And what a better way than to dip my toe into the investment water.

I had set limits for myself as well. If my investment were to go down to $20, I would try to unload the coin or switch it to something else. Also, I had a cap as to when I would give this a serious reevaluation. If the investment rose to $500, I would then look at projections again and see where all the cryptocurrencies I bought parts of were thought to be going. Then I would either cash out, switch to all bitcoin, or to what was growing the fastest. Or, I might just leave things as they are and reevaluate again at $1000 if I would be so lucky as to see that number.

Now, I'm going to tell you during this time of the process of this book, my currency has grown. I now have $178.00 in my wallet. Right now, that's a profit of $78. Of course, this has been an election year, factors have figured into the growth such as the ever growing bitcoin that seems to just keep going up in value. Ethereum is also a coin that does seem to be riding bitcoin's coattails. Again, this is just my personal story. It could have just as easily gone the other way. So, for now, I'm in a holding pattern and watching the numbers and reading numbers.

Does this sound interesting to you? Does it sound fun? You could actually get into cryptocurrency with less than $100. Or you could invest a whole lot more! But in no way are we encouraging that. I have to admit though, this is fun!

Losing money though, is NOT fun. And I could honestly wake up in the morning and every dime could be gone. That's the truth. Every penny could be gone. If I were to cash out and put this money in the bank, it would be guaranteed. There are no guarantees in cryptocurrency! Please remember that!

In the bank or in the stock market, my money would not be growing like it is right now. I would not have the projected growth for January like I am projected to have either. My odds right now look very good for doubling my $100 by Feb 1, 2021. Think if I would have invested $1000, or $10,000? Do you see how some people are really cleaning up in cryptocurrency right now? Wall Street truly does not want this to get out!

If you do decide to invest, do not check your wallet or the boards every day or several times a day! That will make you crazy! It's hard not to do those checks because you can see the dollars going up and down but try to invest and let it be at least for few days. I can honestly say, it is very hard not to watch the money sites live! I am guilty of just sitting here and watching for a few minutes.

How to Spot a Fake Investment Site

This is important. It's a shame we have to deal with this and we hope we have given you enough information that you know which sites to go to should you decide to invest. But there is a big difference from going to Whitehouse.gov and Whitehouse-.net. You have got to check out the domain name that you are going to.

When someone sends you an email advertising something that is always "too good to be true" hit the reply button and then look at what is up in the tool bar. Usually, it is a bogus address to a bogus place. Do not reply to those type of emails. And, a good rule of thumb is, "IF it sounds too good to be true, it probably is!"

Another piece of advice is to not pay for anything with a

direct transfer of funds. Pay with a credit card so your purchase is protected if something should go wrong.

Always know that if there is some kind of large give away, it's too good to be true. Run! Use secure internet connections and do your diligence to figure out who you are dealing with. NEVER check on your funds at an airport or any public place for that matter. Especially an airport.

The exchanges we have listed in this book are reputable. Please consider using those recommended should you decide to invest. Go to those exchanges and check them out. See if you like what they have to say and their introductions. You will find, we have done excellent research on everything written in these pages!

Remember the young man on Reddit who was financially independent in his 20s. You are on your way to knowing how to do what he did by just reading this book. We have given you so much knowledge and tools for your crypto-toolbox! You are on your way should you want to be an investor! Again, this book in no way is encouraging you to invest your money. We are just bringing you education should you decide to invest in cryptocurrency! If you don't want to miss this investment opportunity, we've given you what you need between the pages of The Crypto Generation!

AFTERWORD

Wall Street does not like this book and does not want this book to be read or for you to buy more copies to share with friends!

Inside these pages we have given you the facts of the fastest growing investments in the world and they are not on the New York Stock Exchange!

This has been a fast ride or a fast read, however you want to put it. But if this has been a fast read, then that means you have not been bored. If you cannot wait to get started in the crypto investment game, then this book has inspired you and hopefully you are going into investing in crypto with education because of what you have read between these pages!

Remember, this book was not written to encourage you to invest in any cryptocurrency of any kind. This book was written for your information and entertainment. However, if after reading our information, you feel inspired to invest and also feel like you have more answers than questions, we have done our job. And just maybe it's time for you to jump into the water of cryptocurrency!

As I have said, while just doing the research, I had to invest! And I have already made money. I've learned even more and will invest even more! My friend who bought $700 of bitcoin has made a lot just since mid-December and if the rising trend continues, will make a tidy sum in 2021! A very tidy sum! He will actually probably add to his investment as well before the end of this month! But you do you! This book does not say invest or don't invest. We are bringing you education about cryptocurrencies and the benefits and also the hazards involved.

Of course, as you begin your journey, you will have more things you will want to ask and research. You will probably want to return to the pages of The Crypto Generation more than once for consultation! This book is jam packed with information about cryptocurrency! It's all right here. And there are references here to actual courses you can take for free. No other book or single webpage will do that for you!

Also, in this book we have even included questions people have after reading similar books and we are giving the answers!

You have been able to read more information in this book than if you searched the web for days! You have even found out what happens to your cryptocurrency investment when you die. The Crypto Generation has showed you how to protect this investment and how to keep it from just disappearing. You can share your cryptocurrency with your heirs if you know what you are doing. We have taught you how to do that!

You have learned about the many terms involved in cryptocurrency and how the blockchain works. Terms such as bitcoin, wallet, mining and blockchain among others. We also learned many secondary terms along the way including several altcoins such as Litecoin, Tether, Chainlink, and Ethereum.

You have been taught how to set up a wallet and how to choose an exchange to complete your first purchase. We have outlined several different altcoins and the price of bitcoin to help you decide what you should purchase should you decide to invest in cryptocurrency. Not only that, but we have some expert predictions as to what some of these currencies are "expected" to do. Again, no one knows for sure and we are not in any way encouraging you to invest. We are just putting the facts out there as we know them today!

We know that cryptocurrency investments are transparent because the blockchain records everything that transpires. As long as you hang onto your wallet and keys, your investment is safe and secure. We have given you a small glimpse of predictions into 2021 of what some cryptocurrencies may do during this year. And that is very valuable information if you should decide to invest!

While this form of investment may have been new to you or you may be more experienced, there were many things in this book to learn and to gain from the information. It's up to you what to do with the information you have read! We cannot make promises or give advice, but we can present information! And one piece of information we have passed along is to start small and do your research. Within these pages we have completed our due diligence of cryptocurrency research for you!

Is Cryptocurrency volatile? Most skeptics will tell you it is the most volatile investment risk today. But proponents of cryptocurrency say this investment is the new investment of the future and they believe it will become a method of common exchange. In this book we have showed you ways bitcoin already has been used as a transfer of exchange for goods and services. And bitcoin continues to rise in value as well as other altcoins.

As you have read, you do not have to be able to invest a lot. In fact, some circles believe it is better to start out slow. Even a small investment can yield great dividends. And a large investment can also cause a person to lose quite a bit. However, if you want to go big or go home, some people have gotten rich doing exactly that!

Examine the fun facts and also the facts every investor should know. They are important for you and for your money. Be sure to check out the other developing cryptocurrencies we have listed for you. Any one of these could be the next bitcoin! You never know! Or it could drop right off the chain. Remember, a lot of money can be made and/or lost in cryptocurrency. Choose wisely!

Bottom line, people who are proponents of cryptocurrency tend to sing the crypto-praises, while people who are more cautious about these investments, will flat out tell you it's not solid and to stay away. Most people who like to invest, after being educated, will try at least with a small sum of money to see how they fair with this type of investment. My personal view is that it is fun! I like being able to watch what is going on with my wallet and with what the currencies are doing at any time during the day. Remember, try not to check too often!

Cryptocurrency isn't for everyone. You have to have money you feel is money you can spend! That is first and foremost.

You cannot gamble with money you honestly need to buy groceries. Reread the pages of this book again to really digest some of this material. This new terminology and new way of investing could be an incredible opportunity! It's time to find a way to way to invest where you actually can see your money grow!

You have step by step information about how to invest and how to set up your wallet. We have given you reputable exchanges with which to deal with and who have high marks in value to consumers. We have also taught you how to evaluate cryptocurrencies and how to invest. There are good solid pieces of advice and caution within the pages of this book along with an element of fun that comes with investing!

As this book instructs throughout, do your research and then invest! The value of some cryptocurrency has been known to go up 100% and then plummet down 95% in the same afternoon. It's a wild ride. Do not invest more than you can lose or have fun with! But if you are intrigued to invest in cryptocurrency, maybe you are ready to start Making Money in Cryptocurrency Today!

◆◆◆

While I make no guarantees, in my opinion it is only a matter of time before Bitcoin becomes a more widely used, widely accepted currency, and skyrockets in value. I don't know if Bitcoin will completely replace currency, however I think it will definitely be a payment option that will be accepted by businesses, and used by many individuals.

Also, because of the fact only 21 million Bitcoins will ever be in existence, once the price of Bitcoin stabilizes, Bitcoin will most likely be used as a store of value. Instead of banks or gold, our grandchildren may be putting their savings into Bitcoin. This will be like cash pre-1913, and the detrimental effects of governmental inflation will not decrease the value of hard earned money stored in Bitcoin.

Bitcoin is still quite volatile, but I want you to look at it as a long term investment, and not be too worried about the day-to-day movements. It will most likely have wild swings in the near future, and this is to be expected until it is more widely accepted, and thus stabilizes more. Despite these wild swings, as shown in the logarithmic chart in chapter 4, it is steadily increasing with time.